Women on the Run

—◄O►—

Women on the Run

Janet Campbell Hale

University of Idaho Press
Moscow, Idaho/1999

03 02 01 00 99 5 4 3 2 1

Library of Congress Cataloging-in-Publication Data

Hale, Janet Campbell.
    Women on the run / by Janet Campbell Hale.
        p. cm.
    ISBN 0-89301-217-3 (hardcover : alk. paper)
    1. United States—Social life and customs—20th cen-
tury—Fiction. 2. Indian women—North America—Fiction.
3. Indians of North America—Fiction. 4. Women—United
States—Fiction. I Title.
    PS3558.A3567W66   1999
    813'.54—dc21   99-20018
                                                        CIP

—◄O►—

Dedicated to the Memory of
Doris Hunt Dolan, 1930-1994

Thanks to The National Endowment for the Arts, the Carnegie Fund for Authors, and to the Idaho Commission on the Arts for the fellowships that enabled me to keep the wolf away from my door while writing.

Contents

Claire

A person has to watch her step when she is an inmate of an old people's home. Especially if her mind happens to be clear. Especially if she loathes the so-called home and resents the son who brought her to Oakland, California, who insisted, after his father died three years ago, that she live with him. "Come home with us, Ma," he said. "You can't live all alone out in the country. We love you. We would love having you. Let us look after you." (She was grief-stricken at the time; after all, she and Sam, who were married some fifty odd years, were as close as two people could be.) Her mind was clouded when she agreed to leave Idaho and its harsh climate for sunny California, when she agreed to leave her home and everything that had ever meant anything to her, even her dog. At the time it seemed the rational thing to do.

She *was* old, after all, at seventy-six. (Now she was three years older.) And it was true that the winters were hard and she didn't know how she would manage without Sam. And then there was the case a year or two before of the old widow who was beaten to death by a gang of teenagers. The girl who testified against the others in exchange for immunity told how they knocked at the old woman's door and asked to use her telephone. Their car had broken down, they told her, and they needed to call a tow truck. The old woman let them in and, turning her back to them, said, "The phone is in here. Just follow me." One of the girls stabbed the old woman in the back, but she braced herself in a doorway and didn't fall. The girl pulled the knife out of the first wound and stabbed her again. This time she fell and the other girls began kicking her and pounding her with their fists as she, realizing now what was happening, began to pray: "The Lord is my shepherd, I shall not want." She was dead before she could finish her prayer.

That heinous crime had occurred in the next county less than a hundred miles from Claire's home. They did it, the one who testified said, because they wanted to see what it felt like to kill someone, and they had decided, some weeks before, that their victim would be either a young child or an elderly person. The weekend before they'd gone to Northtown Mall in Spokane hoping to find a child who was not being watched carefully whom they could lure away. No luck there. They didn't know the old woman who became their victim, whose name was Mrs. Olson, but their school bus passed her house twice a day on school days. They'd seen her working in her garden and sitting on her front porch. They'd never seen anyone else with her and figured she must live alone. Elderly widows who live alone aren't unusual.

"Remember poor Mrs. Olson," Claire's son, Ozzie, had said, and that was enough, finally, to make up her mind. But Maybelle never wanted her mother-in-law in her home. After she found Claire's journal, she wanted her out.

Claire began keeping a journal about a month after she first came to her son's home. She was used to Sam, to telling him her most intimate thoughts, telling him what she had seen or heard and what her impressions were. Without Sam she found her thoughts floating away before she got a good look at them. At first her journals were a substitute for the good company she was used to. She talked to her journal, that is, to herself, rather than to no one at all. The journal-writing gave her a sense of control. Her life otherwise was so much out of her control now that she'd become dependent upon her son and his wife.

Maybelle had gone into her room, she said, to give it a more thorough cleaning than Claire was obviously capable of giving it. And she found the journals right there in the top dresser drawer in ten brightly colored spiral notebooks. Claire's writing was, according to Maybelle, "Full of bitching and pissing and moaning." (Maybelle was *not* the most refined woman in the Bay Area.) "She doesn't like our house. She called our walls Pepto Bismol pink. She doesn't like California. It's too crowded and she misses the

◄○►
Claire

seasons. Hah! What an ingrate your mother is! After we opened our home to her." Maybelle issued an ultimatum to Ozzie: "Either she goes or I go!" Of course Claire was the one who went.

"I was a fool to have listened to you, Ozzie," she said to her son on the drive to Loma Vista. "I would prefer returning to my own home."

"Don't start in, Ma. You know you can't live alone. You need someone to look after you full time now. Remember poor Mrs. Olson."

Ozzie, the eldest of her three boys, was no spring chicken himself. His hairline receded just a bit and he had a double chin and a pot belly. A high school and college football player, he had gone to fat in middle age. He was a grandfather himself now. "It's okay, Ozzie. I'll be better off in the home." She was never that fond of Maybelle, and no doubt Maybelle knew. She wondered why Ozzie hadn't married a girl from back home or one of the girls who was his college classmate instead of a brassy blond white girl who worked at a hamburger stand near the UCLA campus. But then who was she to question Ozzie's odd choice?

Now, firmly ensconced at Loma Vista, Claire knew better than to rock the boat in any way. She kept no journal as there was even less privacy than at Ozzie's. She tried to keep quiet and cause no stir, to be as unobtrusive as she could be. She didn't want anyone to know how she felt. She could end up like one or the other of the McIvers.

Henry and Martha McIver were the only married couple she ever encountered at Loma Vista. Mr. McIver didn't try to hide his anger. "We were doing just fine, Martha and me, on our own. Our son just got tired of waiting for us to pass away and decided to put us here and grab control of our house and land, while he's still young enough to enjoy it. We were fine. Our grandson came every other Saturday to help with the yard work and any heavy lifting we needed to have done. True, my driver's license was revoked last year because my vision and reflexes aren't that good anymore, but we don't need to drive. Our neighbors give us lifts into town. The supermarket delivers for seniors. Sonny Boy has another thing coming if he thinks he can get away with this!" McIver's lawyer paid him a couple of visits at the home (he was going to sue the son and he was going to sue Loma Vista Nursing Home, he said, for false imprisonment).

━◦━
Claire

But the thing was, McIver was eighty-nine, and no matter how lucid of mind or spry of body, no court would rule in his favor . . . no court would agree with him that he would be fine living on his own. And then there was Martha. Though "only" eighty, Martha, beginning shortly after the birth of their only child, frequently suffered from depression and now began to show signs of senility.

One day their grandson told Henry he worried about them. His father was worried, too, that the old people couldn't manage on their own anymore.

To set his mind at ease, Henry confided in the young man.

"No need to worry none about us. None at all. See, your grandmother and I know we're getting on and it might come to our not being able to manage. We made a pact. If the going gets too rough and it appears we can't handle it anymore, well, keep it to yourself now, don't mention it to your dad, but we decided we're going to check out together. Not some hideous way, now, so don't be afraid of any 'grisly finds,' but easy-like. Get in our car in the garage and start the motor. Take some pills. Just go to sleep. Something real easy-like. So don't worry about us." The grandson did tell their son. All in all, it didn't seem likely to Claire that any judge would find in Henry's and Martha's favor.

"And when we get out of here, one of the first things I'm going to do is sue this damned place for false imprisonment!" Henry said.

Martha didn't carry on like Henry. (Didn't "bitch" as Maybelle would say.) She paced the floor and wrung her hands and refused to eat. She hyperventilated, and then they made her take deep, slow breaths into a paper bag.

"The poor dear," Mrs. Lacey, one of the attendants told Claire. "He's got her all upset with his rantin' and ravin'. He's got some attitude that one. Well, I'll let you in on a little secret, Miz LaFromme, he ain't gonna be kept here much longer, the old coot. We're gettin' rid of 'im! See how he likes them apples!" And they did get rid of him, striking in the middle of the night with no warning.

"They came into our room and told him he was run down and needed a vitamin shot," Martha told Claire the morning following her husband's abduction. "He said no he didn't want a shot of anything, and they were nuts if they thought he believed for one split second that they had vitamins there. He was no fool. They held him down and forced it on him, him cussing them out all the while."

"Get the hell away from me, you bloody gorillas," Claire had heard him yell, no doubt at the Santos brothers. The burly Santoses' arms were all covered with thick black hair. Of course old McIver had no hope of fighting them off. They sedated him and then carried him away on a stretcher.

"When I asked them where they were taking my husband they just said, 'Someplace else.' I don't know how I'll live without him."

"Oh, you'll do just fine without that cantankerous old bugger," Mrs. Lacey, who was in Claire's room making beds, said. Claire wanted to say something smart like, "Who asked you, you old bugger?" but she didn't dare say a word. Matilda, her roommate who died recently, sometimes talked back to them and she suffered for it. They wouldn't answer her when she clicked the red button that lit a light at the desk signaling she needed assistance. They often didn't bring her meal tray until last when the food was cold.

And if she spoke to them they would ignore her as if she were invisible and inaudible. They wrote reports and stuck them in her file and gave them to her children to read when they visited, and Matilda's children would confront her as though she were a bad little girl. "So you've been giving them a hard time here. Shame on you! When are you going to straighten yourself up and act right?" they'd demand and Matilda, her face flushed, would look down at the floor.

Claire knew better than to speak her mind at Loma Vista. She took comfort in thinking they—Mrs. Lacey, the Santos Brothers, and the mean head nurse—would be old themselves one day. Mrs. Lacey and the head nurse were already middle-aged. They were not creating good karma for their old ages. They would suffer for their meanness to the helpless elderly under their care. But Claire wouldn't be around to see it.

At night Martha cried in her sleep making odd yowling sounds, like a cougar.

"Good Lord Almighty," Mrs. Sullivan, Claire's new roommate, said when she heard. "What on earth is that? Sounds like a damned banshee!"

"That's just poor Martha in the next room crying in her sleep. She can't help it."

"Can't help it, eh? We'll see about that! I'm talking to the management. It's outrageous. Medicare and my son and daughter aren't paying out good money so that I will be kept awake by shrieking. Poor little Martha isn't going to get away with it."

After that night the yowling stopped. Claire wondered how Martha controlled herself. Maybe, she thought, Martha kept herself awake all night. They were all fearful, or should be (including Mrs. Sullivan, though she didn't realize it yet), of rocking the boat. They were, after all, powerless, and it didn't pay to make waves.

Four days after McIver's abduction, Martha somehow made it past all the watchful eyes on floors one, two, and three to the roof. Claire wondered whether Martha dove off the roof, then, as soon as she arrived, or did she take in the view for a minute or two (but she would have been wary of being caught), did she hesitate before taking the leap, did she have to work up her nerve? Or was it easy for her . . . did she have the heart for it? Did she do it with surety that that was the right thing, the only reasonable thing to do? Martha jumped. Or dove. Or stepped off the roof into the air.

Claire happened to be standing at her window looking out at that moment. She saw Martha pass her window. It was very, very sudden and there was no scream; she made no sound of any kind. Claire saw the body hit the ground and heard the "thud" it made upon impact.

Later, after the ambulance took the corpse away, Claire snuck out into the courtyard. She knelt on the grass beside the spot where Martha had landed. Such a small person, yet she had left an impression on the ground. The grass lay flattened. Claire pressed the palm of her hand into the impression. "Now you're free, Martha dear," she whispered.

"Hey, you crazy old bat, what do you think you're doing," Mrs. Lacey grabbed her roughly by the arm and pulled her to her feet. It reminded her of the nuns when she was a little girl back on the reservation and forced to go to Catholic mission school. The nuns treated children like that, grabbing, manhandling, scolding. She never dreamed she would spend her old age in the same way she had spent most of her childhood, under lock and key, keeping her guard up at all times, being rudely spoken to and physically abused. Mrs. Lacey pulled and pushed, all the while scolding. "You know better than that Miz LaFromme. You know good and well you're not allowed outside without supervision. I'm going to have to file a report on you now. And, of course, your son will be told. We'll tell your son you're not to be trusted, you sneaky little thing, you damned old weasel you. Just about had me fooled, but you're like all the rest. Can't trust a one of ya' damned coots."

That was when she first heard her own voice whispering: *"You've got to get out of this place. If it's the last thing you ever do."* Yes. But how? Probably every inmate of Loma Vista had heard at one time or another that same voice in their head, their own voice saying the same thing. Did anyone ever succeed in running away, she wondered? *"You've got to get out of this place!"* it said again, no longer a mere whisper, but with conviction.

"Yes," she agreed silently. *"Yes."*

Ozzie visited her every first Sunday of the month. When he came again she brought the subject up.

"I wish I had never let you talk me into leaving home, son. I would have been all right. I had Mike. You know Mike is a good dog." Mike was their young Doberman whom Sam had trained to attack anyone who might threaten them. But he could be gentle, too. She'd given Mike to her nephew, Joe Whitehawk, and his little boy, Billy, when she left Idaho.

"Don't start in, Ma. We've been over this a dozen times. No old lady can live out in the country all alone."

"Well, some do."

"And some are found dead in their houses."

"Everyone dies. Better to die in my own house I would think than . . ."

"Ma! That's enough! You must have someone to look after you. That's all there is to it."

She thought of telling him about the death of her last roommate, before Mrs. Sullivan. Matilda—Mrs. Krenshaw—who had shared Claire's room for two years.

The last night of her life Matilda took very ill. Claire went over and touched her forehead. "You're burning up!" she said. Matilda shivered so hard her sheet and blanket slipped off. Her eyes rolled back. "I'm going to get help, Matilda." Her friend opened her eyes a moment and seemed to focus on Claire's face.

"You can't go home in this storm, Grace," Matilda said. "I'll tell the boys to bed your horses down and I'll get you some bedding." Matilda was delirious. Claire hated to leave her and clicked first Matilda's red button, and then, when the staff didn't respond, her own. Still they didn't answer and did not appear. She replaced the blanket and sheet, covering her friend though she knew they would be shivered off again right away.

Claire walked to the desk and told them Mrs. Krenshaw was seriously ill. They acted as though they hadn't heard her. She thought of calling an ambulance but knew there would be big trouble for both Matilda and herself if she dared do that.

Claire stayed by Matilda's side. She soaked washcloths in cold water and put them on Matilda's forehead and replaced them when they warmed with fresh cold ones. She wished she had aspirin to give her. That would bring the fever down, but they weren't allowed to have any sort of medications at Loma Vista except for what was doled out by the staff several times a day. "Don't leave me, Grace. I'm frightened," Matilda said reaching out. Claire took her hand and held it, patted it. She knew Grace was Matilda's sister who had died in childbirth many, many years ago.

"Don't worry. I'm here. I won't leave. I'm right here." About three A.M., when Matilda hadn't spoken for an hour, Claire heard the death rattle. She wondered why it was called that. It was more like a gurgle than a rattle. Anyway she knew what it meant. Matilda opened her eyes and looked at Claire. Claire felt that Matilda recognized her this time. Then she closed her eyes and was gone.

Claire went to the front desk and told the fat, freckle-faced, red-haired black nurse on duty that Mrs. Krenshaw had passed away. "We don't have time for that now," she said, irritated that Claire was bugging her. She'd been reading a book, which Claire could tell by the cover illustration of an extremely handsome man embracing a very attractive young woman in a low-cut gown was a cheap romance. Maybelle, her daughter-in-law, devoured such books. "Go back to bed!"

Just before they brought the breakfast trays, around seven o'clock, the Santos brothers finally came and got Mrs. Krenshaw's dead body and took it away. That's how they looked after old people at Loma Vista Nursing Home.

"Look, Granny Claire," Buddy, Ozzie's grandson, said holding up a new crayon drawing, "do you like it?" Buddy, who was eight, usually came with Ozzie. Her *tupiya*.* The one bright spot in all of this was that she had gotten to know her *tupiya*. Buddy, who was very fair-skinned, had dark brown curly hair and large grey-hazel eyes. No one would ever take him for an Indian. It didn't matter. He was her dear *tupiya*.

* Coeur d'Alene Salish meaning both "great-grandparent" and "great-grandchild."

"Bring it here, let's have a look." She blinked back her tears.

The drawing appeared to be of two people sitting in a giant cup which was on a giant saucer. One figure wore a baseball cap, the other had two long braids. Both wore wide grins. She and Buddy were often the subjects of his drawings. "Is that us?" he nodded. "Why are we sitting in a cup? Is someone going to drink us?"

"No. We're at Disneyland and here we're riding The Mad Hatter's Tea Party. Next we're going to Pirates of the Caribbean."

"We sure look happy."

"We are."

"Ma, I have to go make a phone call, okay. I'll be back in a few minutes. You stay with your Gran, Buddy."

"His *tupiya*," Claire corrected her son, who ignored her.

"Okay," Buddy said. As soon as Ozzie left the room, Buddy said in a very quiet voice, just barely above a whisper, "Gran, I have something to tell you. Don't tell nobody, okay? I've got a plan."

"Okay."

"When I grow up, I'm going to come here and break you out."

"How will you do that?"

"I'll bring a disguise of some kind. We'll walk right out the front door. Then we'll run away. They'll never find us."

"Where will we go, Buddy?"

"I don't know. I was thinking maybe L.A."

"Why L.A.?"

"Because it's far away. Because it's real big. And because it's close to Disneyland. After I get a job we'll go to Disneyland on my days off. We'll have a good time."

"Sounds good to me, Buddy. Sounds great. And thanks. I feel better now knowing I'm not going to be stuck in this place forever." Buddy smiled. One of his front teeth was missing. Maybe he wasn't eight. Maybe he was seven.

◄○►
Claire

That was the second time she heard her own voice saying, *"You've got to get out of this place. And you're going to have to do it all yourself. Nobody is going to rescue you. You can't wait for Buddy to grow up. You have to do it, Claire. You're all you've got."*

Yes. She already knew. *She* was all she had.

"I love that picture of us in a teacup, Bud. You know what, I'm not going to tape this one to the wall. I'm going to keep it in my pocket so I can take it out and look at it whenever I want." One wall was covered with Buddy's drawings. Mrs. Sullivan said they were an eyesore and when Claire refused to take them down, Mrs. Sullivan said she was going to complain, was going to change rooms if she had to. Claire was making waves. She was afraid of being taken away in the night as Henry McIver was to "someplace else." Claire had to get out.

That very evening, just before dinner was brought in, Claire stole into the room of a man named Arthur. "Hi, Arthur. How're you doing?"

Arthur narrowed his watery eyes and looked her up and down.

"What do you want?" he asked. He was a skinny little man about her size.

"I want to borrow some clothes from you, okay?" Claire said, opening the old man's locker. So spare and neat.

Arthur was not in his right mind, like many, perhaps most, of the inmates of Loma Vista. He saw goblins and giant nuns and rodeo clowns traipsing around his room at odd hours. Sometimes he thought he was still a soldier in France. Sometimes he thought he was a young husband and father and talked about his kids and his job at the factory. Some days Arthur thought he was in a POW camp and would refuse to speak at all except to give his name, rank, and serial number.

Nobody would believe Arthur if he told them Claire had come into his room, opened his locker door, selected a sports coat, a pair of trousers, a cotton dress shirt, and a vee-neck pullover sweater (all of which she knew were there since she'd seen him decked out in these clothes when his children came to visit, which was only once a year at Christmas). And besides, he didn't appear to recognize her today. Maybe he thought she was an enemy solider.

Arthur's clothes fit her nicely, except for the shoes, which were much too big. Damn! Well, she had a pair of walking shoes, no heels, very plain. Maybe they would pass for men's shoes.

She took the folded crayon drawing Bud had given her, the one depicting the two of them happily riding in giant cups at Disneyland, and put it in the inside pocket of the sports coat.

Claire decided she would make her break after they collected the dinner trays. They were busy then and wouldn't be around again until late evening. And her cantankerous roommate, Mrs. Sullivan, always took a bath after dinner.

The dinner trays were brought. Mrs. Sullivan ate her dinner. Then she took a clean towel from her locker, a bar of soap, her robe. Claire couldn't let her leave just yet. She needed Mrs. Sullivan to be gone right after the trays were collected. She had to dress, then make good her escape. Timing was important.

"Mrs. Sullivan, tell me, are you sleeping well now?" Mrs. Sullivan frowned at her.

"Why, yes, I am. Thank you. And I don't think I'm to blame, not at all, for your friend's death. She was the one who chose to jump off the roof. I was within my rights complaining about that horrid noise she made at night."

"Of course, Mrs. Sullivan. Of course. Nobody thinks you're to blame. You need your rest. We all do." Mrs. Sullivan left the room as the attendant swept in and swept the trays away. Claire closed the door behind them. She couldn't lock it, though. Loma Vista doors had no locks on them. She dressed quickly in Arthur's clothes and her leather walking shoes and looked at her reflection. "Not bad, if I do say so myself," she said. She looked like a man, except for the long braids. They might be a giveaway down here. You didn't see men, like up on the reservation, in long braids. Maybe she could get a hat somewhere and pin them up under it. For now, though, she was ready. This was it.

The upper half of the window opened outward. She was very slim and, for an old person, very agile. She made it out onto the ledge. Though they were on the first floor, still, it was about a twenty foot drop. She got down on her knees and got hold of the ledge with both hands and let her body slide down the outer wall. This way it was only about a ten foot drop and, with any luck, she would fall into the flower beds where the earth was damp and soft. She did. She kept close to the ground and to the building. She cut across a park and kept walking.

She could feel and hear her heart pounding. Her body, sensing her excitement, sent adrenaline to her aid to help her out. Fight or flight. She would rather take flight than put up a fight. Oh, the giddiness! The exhilaration!

Claire spent her first night of freedom under a park bench beside Lake Merrit. She didn't get much rest; it was too cold and damp and she was too excited. Towards daybreak she did doze off for just a short while, an hour or forty-five minutes. But she couldn't let them find her sleeping under a park bench.

It was time to wake up, go downtown, find a pawn broker, and sell her diamond ring. But it would be a couple of hours yet before the stores opened.

She thought of Buddy. If she were successful in her escape, she would, most likely, never see Buddy again. What would he think when he passed the nursing home on his way to school this morning and saw that she wasn't there waiting for his smile and wave as she did every weekday morning? She decided she would double back a bit and try to see Buddy one last time, try to intercept him on his way to school. She didn't even know where his school was located exactly. She would have to take a chance.

She waited under a tall palm tree in front of a modern, boxy apartment complex of pink stucco. This was just four blocks west of Loma Vista. She tried not to look suspicious.

Loma Vista, housed in a dingy grey concrete-block structure, loomed on a high hill, dominating the landscape. In its dark-grey ugliness it could have been a penitentiary, but one without high walls topped by barbed wire and towers with armed guards. A house of detention for those who committed the crime of getting old. Loma Vista's inmates were *all* on death row with no possibility of a last minute reprieve.

"God! I did it! I got away! I got away!" She spotted her *tupiya* walking towards her. He carried his little tin lunch bucket with Batman's likeness on it. (He'd taken it to the nursing home on one of his visits, when it was new, and showed it to her.) He wore a green-and-yellow baseball cap.

◄○►
Claire

Her heart warmed at the sight of him. He was right in front of her when he looked up into her eyes and realized who she was. He smiled, "Grandma Claire! It's you!"

"Shhh! Don't draw attention! I'll walk you to your school. Let's go." And they began walking. How odd. They'd never walked down the street together until now.

"Did you escape? Your disguise is boss! Here, take my cap," he said and handed it to her. She took it and put it on her head. "Perfect fit!"

"Yeah. Now, tuck your braids up under your cap, Gram. There! Now you *really* look like a guy!" The old woman disguised as a man and her now bare-headed great-grandson held hands as they walked briskly down the street on the chilly late summer morning.

In front of the red-brick school the boy hugged her around the waist. She stroked his hair. She almost wept. She loved this little boy so, whom she'd never seen until she came to California with Ozzie and Maybelle. Something good and important had come out of the California fiasco. "I love you, Gran," Buddy said. "Be careful."

"I love you, too, Buddy. And I want you to know I took the last drawing you did for me, of us at Disneyland, you know the one, and just as soon as I get where I'm going I'm going to take it out and tape it to my wall. Don't worry about me. I'm going to be fine. Okay?"

"Okay. And you don't worry about me neither, okay?"

"Okay." Then he went his way and she went hers. Her eyes welled up with tears, but she blinked them back and shed not one. She had to be tough to pull this one off and she was. *"I'm a tough old bird,"* she thought to herself. *"A tough old bird. And I'm going to make it."*

The man at the pawn shop near the Greyhound depot would give her only $100 for her diamond ring. "It's worth at least $2,000," she said.

➤◯➤
Claire

"Hey! You come waltzing in here with a diamond ring and no I.D. whatsoever and $100 isn't good enough for you? That's my offer, Pops. $100 and no questions asked. Take it or leave it." Claire took it.

She went to the Greyhound depot and purchased a ticket on the local to San Francisco. The important thing now was getting out of town as quickly as possible. If Ozzie or the nursing home were looking for her, they would be checking the buslines for an old woman buying a ticket to Idaho or Washington, and they would be looking for her in Oakland, not San Francisco. She wasn't sticking around.

She had only a ten-minute wait before boarding time. She bought a newspaper and sat down on a bench. She noticed a small wool blanket, blue and green plaid, neatly folded on the bench beside her. She picked it up. She decided to keep it rather than turn it in to lost and found. She could use a blanket. She hoped whoever had forgotten it and left it behind didn't need it too badly.

In San Francisco she bought herself a one-way ticket to Portland, Oregon, and then sat reading her paper and waiting for an hour to pass. Dear Abby was one of her favorite features. *"Dear Abby: I am in love with a wonderful man. I have never been in love before although I am thirty-three. I was my invalid mother's caretaker from the time I graduated high school until last year when she died. When I met my man, I was a thirty-two-year-old virgin. When we had been going together for about six months, he told me he was married and had two young children. As soon as his kids start school, he says, he'll move out of the house and begin divorce proceedings. He hasn't made love with his wife, who is frigid, in well over a year. He actually began weeping as he told me I was the love of his life, that he never imagined he'd ever love anyone so much. He is very religious and believes God gave us to each other. My friends tell me to get out, that he's a low-life and has no intention of getting divorced and marrying me. I love him so much, Abby. I am not sure I want to go on without him. Please help me. Signed, Starved-for-Love in Kansas City."*

Claire noticed two policemen enter the big waiting room. It was eleven o'clock now and the large depot was very crowded. The cops took a turn around the depot checking things out while Claire pretended to read her paper and furtively watched them. They woke a white-haired bag lady and told her she had to move on. She did. At the door the bag lady paused and looked back before stepping out onto the street. For just a moment she and Claire made eye contact. Claire wondered how it was the bag lady, nearly as old as she, was allowed to live on her own. No children, she guessed, or at least none who were concerned about her. "Get along there, Granny. Don't wanna have to run you in," one of the young cops called to the bag lady, who went on her way, pushing her supermarket cart full of paper and plastic bags. The cops didn't give Claire a second look.

"Dear 'Starved-for-Love,'" Abby's reply began, *"Not everyone, including me, would agree with you that this man is a 'wonderful guy.' He deceived you. He's cheating on his wife. And don't buy that baloney about no sex in over a year. Get rid of the bum! At first it will be painful, but in the long run you'll like your-self better. The world is full of 'wonderful guys.' Unfortunately, your boyfriend's not one of them."*

Claire would hate to have Abby's job. What if "Starved-for-Love in Kansas City" gave the wonderful guy the boot and then found herself utterly bereft and ended up committing suicide? After all, she'd led a terribly sheltered life. She didn't have experience that would teach her pain would pass and life would go on. Maybe that rat of a married man was her only source of love ever.

Claire would hate to have Abby's job, but she wished she had a job of some kind. Who would hire a person her age to do anything? If she drew on Sam's social security benefits, Ozzie would find her and take her back to lockup. Where would she get money? How would she live? *"Focus on the moment, on the road ahead. You are alive and you are free.*" At the moment her most pressing problem was a full bladder. First things first.

Not without some apprehension, Claire went to the men's room. She was not surprised to see two men standing at urinals holding their penises and relieving themselves. Claire chose one of the two booths that had doors, but, bad luck, it had no lock. She had to hold the door closed with one hand as she sat on the toilet. "*Kway Elpsh!*" she muttered under her breath. Then, aware she had just spoken the only Coeur d'Alene Salish she'd heard in a few years, she said it again, whispering: "Kway Elpsh!" (*"A fine thing I must say!"* she would have said in English were she speaking English.)

When she came out of the little stall with a door that did not latch, she washed her hands. She still wore her gold wedding ring on the third finger of her left hand. Above it, where the diamond ring had encircled her finger for so long, the skin was much lighter, almost white. It showed something important was missing. Nobody looked at her. Nobody at all. It worked! She was a smashing success. She looked at herself in the mirror. She didn't make a bad looking old coot if she did think so herself. She smiled at her reflection. "*We got out of that place, old man, We did it!*"

The coach bound for Portland pulled out of the stall and headed down Mission Street to the freeway entry and crossed the Bay Bridge and stopped at the Oakland depot to take on more passengers. Claire didn't see Ozzie or any police.

A fat middle-aged woman boarded and took the aisle seat beside her.

How thrilling to sail up the road so fast and so free! Everything she saw, the other vehicles, the green hills, the green pastures full of black-and-white spotted cows, all of it was a feast for her eyes! It was as if she had stirred to life again after a long, cold winter's hibernation.

Claire

"Pretty day, isn't it," the woman beside her said. Claire nodded. It was. Clear, incredible blue clarity. A pretty day. "My name is June. What's your name?"

Claire, who had always had a deep voice, answered, "Jack."

"How do you do, Jack. Are you going all the way to Portland?" Claire nodded. "Me too. I live in San Francisco. I'm going to Portland to see my daughter. She's going to have a baby. My first grandchild. I'm going to stay on and help her for awhile. Imagine! Me, a grandmother. Hey, do you have grandchildren? Of course, you must. And you probably have great-grandchildren as well, don't you, Jack," Claire nodded again. "Do you live in Portland or are you going there to visit?"

"Live there."

"Oh, do you live alone or do you stay with relatives?"

"Alone."

"Imagine that! At your age! I admire independence. I couldn't help noticing your high cheekbones, Jack. Are you Native American?" Claire nodded again.

"What tribe? Do you say tribe? What tribe do you belong to, Jack?" Claire turned her back on gabby June and said, mumbled, in a deep, manlike (she hoped) voice, "Sleepy. Gonna sleep now."

In Portland June's pregnant daughter and a tall lanky man, probably her son-in-law, met June. Nobody met Claire, of course. She got off the bus and bought herself a hotdog and coke. Such a long time since she ate anything like that. She slathered mustard onto the dog and wolfed it down. Then she got a chili dog with extra onions and ate it slowly, savoring the intensity. Food at Loma Vista was bland. Many believed old people liked bland food because they had lost their sense of taste. When she was done eating she bought a ticket to Sunnyside, Washington, because the bus to the Yakima Valley was boarding right away and Sunnyside was the first town in the Valley.

Claire couldn't turn her worries off anymore as the bus sped through the night. What would she do? Where would she go? What was going to become of her now that she was free? Her throat constricted. She couldn't go to her own home. Ozzie had rented it to a non-Indian family. The rent helped pay the bills at Loma Vista. Her anxiety grew. Was she insane? A near octogenarian running off like some kid. A kid would lie about their age and sometimes that might work. Maybe Claire could lie about hers, too. How young might she pass for? Nobody ever told her she looked young for her age. Even the rude and nosey June, who was fooled concerning her gender, implied she saw her as a very old person—*"You must have great-grandchildren."* But she wasn't trying to look young. What could she do to make herself look young? Cut her hair for starters. Buy some fashionable, youthful looking clothes. Maybe she could dye her hair. It was snow white now, so she could color it whatever shade she wanted and it would take. People always say black, once her natural color, is too harsh for elderly people even if black had once been their natural color. Maybe medium brown would work. And a little makeup. Maybe she could doll herself up and pass for sixty. What sort of job could a sixty-year-old with no job skills or employment record expect to get? Not a great one.

When the bus stopped, still in Oregon, a couple of hours before entering the Yakima Valley, Claire got off, taking her plaid blanket, and didn't get back on again. She had no desire to go to Sunnyside, and getting off would help confuse anyone who might be looking for her. Biggs Junction this place was called, a wide spot in the road where busses coming and going from all kinds of destinations and points of departure across the Northwest stopped to let off and take on passengers. All Biggs Junction consisted of, though, was a trailer house bus depot, a little cafe, a gas station that was also a repair garage, and a small grocery store.

She sat an hour or so in the depot reading a newspaper. President Kennedy was getting tough with the Russians. Something about Cuba. If push comes to shove, Kennedy would be no pushover. Maybe another war. There were always wars, weren't there? Her horoscope, she was a Capricorn, said "Romance on the horizon but stars do not favor travel. Best stay home today and for the next few days, Cap." She dozed off a little now and then. Finally she toppled over, lying on her side on the bench, and went to sleep.

She dreamed. *She was at Loma Vista where she lay unable to sleep while Mrs. Sullivan snored away in the bed beside her. White moonlight filled the room. She had a heavy heart as she often did at Loma Vista. Her world was one of bleak desolation. She was strong and healthy for a person her age and her mind was clear and sharp, but what was the point? Where was she going? Why was she here? What had she now to look forward to? She'd had such an odd dream, she thought, the night before: that she stole some clothes from Arthur and disguised as a man ran away. But it was just a dream. Just a dream. She'd never be free again.*

Just then Martha McIver opened the door to her room. "Martha!"

"Shhh," Martha said, holding an index finger to her lips. Oh, yes, of course, we mustn't wake Mrs. Sullivan. Martha walked over to Claire's bed, sat down on the chair beside it, and took Claire's hand.

Whispering, Claire said, "Martha! How are you? I thought you were . . . gone." Martha shook her head no. "That's what I wanted them to think. I wanted them to think I was dead so they would send me away in an ambulance. That was a fake ambulance, a rented ambulance. Mr. McIver and some friends of his pretended to be a driver and couple of paramedics. Hah! Joke's on them! I'm better off now, Claire, and happy. Mr. McIver and I are together again. I just wanted to tell you good-bye and let you know I'm not really dead. And neither are you, dear. Remember that."

Claire felt so sad. She began to weep as Martha McIver faded away, "Don't leave me again, Martha," but Martha kept fading until she disappeared.

"Sir. Sir. Wake up, sir. Wake up." It was daylight and a janitor gently nudged her shoulder. "Having a bad dream?" Claire nodded.

"Yes," she said in her deepened, faint voice. "Thank you for waking me."

Claire bought a few supplies: matches, a can opener, some cans of ravioli and corned beef hash, a package of hotdogs, a six-pack of soda pop. She read the headlines on a newspaper. Elizabeth Taylor announces her intention to divorce Eddie Fisher and wed Richard Burton. *"About time,"* Claire thought. The news photo showed a very fat Liz. Fat as she was, she was still beautiful. Probably she'd still be beautiful when she was eighty.

Claire took the newspaper, too, and off she went down into the ditch next to the road, under the fence, and up the side of a grassy, yellow hill. On and on she hiked farther and farther from Biggs Junction and the highway.

At length she found an old tree that cast a big shadow and there she sat, leaning her back against the gnarled, rough bark as she took a deep breath of fresh, free air. She took a can of soda pop from the six-pack and drank it down. Never had soda pop tasted so fine. At last she was truly, truly free. She needed to be alone awhile, she decided. Alone and not having to watch her step or look over her shoulder for the first time since she left Idaho nearly four years before. Decompress. Breathe fresh air. Be alone in her new freedom. She took hold of a branch and broke it down to the appropriate length to make a walking stick for herself.

For several hours she walked, aided by her fine new walking stick, leisurely taking in the scenery, which was mostly desert. Once she spotted a rattlesnake curled up near a pile of boulders. He blended in quite nicely there. Rattlesnakes were okay, she thought. This one held himself still as could be. He thought she didn't see him. He would not strike at her unless she came near enough to step on him. She had no intention of going near him.

Garter snakes, the little black things with yellow or red stripes down their backs, the non-poisonous "good" snakes that ate pests were the kind she didn't like. They were always darting around imposing their presence on humans as though they didn't know they were repulsive, as though they thought themselves cute. Rattlers weren't like that at all. They knew how to keep their distance.

When she came to the top of a high hill and saw a winding creek way down yonder, she headed for it and found a good camping place. She took off her clothes and washed her underpants and shirt and pullover sweater and draped them over bushes to dry. She took the elastic fasteners off the ends of her braids and undid them. Her hair fell loose about her shoulders and down to her waist in back.

She waded out just a few feet into the icy cold river, until the water was knee-deep, then she sat down in a spot that had few stones and bathed herself and rinsed her hair.

Oh, the water was so cold it made her teeth chatter. As soon as she felt clean enough, she waded back out of the water and lay on her back on a smooth, flat rock that was very warm. She spread her white hair all around her to dry in the sun. She felt the sun and warm chinook wind on her naked body and laughed a little to herself. This was so fine, this moment, so fine. All was perfect, absolutely perfect. She was alive again and was glad. Life could be good. No, it *is* good. Despite everything, despite heartache and loss and meanness and unfairness and the fact that we all must die, life is good and in these perfect moments we know the goodness.

Such times occurred most often, it seemed, when she was a child. Once, seventy-one years ago, she was perfectly content a whole summer.

Claire was a little girl of seven when the men from the government took her and hauled her away to Catholic mission school, where she was forced to learn to speak English and to read and write and learn about white people's manners and way of life and about Jesus and the Virgin Mary. That was the year after her mother died.

She hated mission school. Most of the children did, but some seemed to adapt easily. Years later when she was one of the "big girls" (thirteen or fourteen) she heard a boy had hung himself in the dormitory and told his friend he would rather be dead than be a white man's Indian.

They weren't allowed to speak their own language at mission school. If they did and were caught, they would be whipped by the priest.

She hated the food. She especially hated spinach, which, if she actually downed it, made her vomit. The nuns, knowing she hated spinach, would watch her the days spinach was on the menu and force her to take a bite of it before she could eat anything else. She would sit with her mouth full of spinach until the meal was over and the children filed out of the dining hall and then spit it out on the ground. And the nuns forced them to drink milk, never catching on that Indians lack the enzyme to digest it. They all, or almost all, had chronic diarrhea because of the milk.

Most of all she hated the nuns who acted like jailkeepers, who acted much the way the attendants at Loma Vista acted towards those who were under their care and at their mercy.

When Claire had been at mission school a whole school year, she found out the children would not be allowed to return to their homes for summer, but would have to stay there and take piano lessons and learn how to embroider and work in the laundry and kitchen and scrub the floors on their hands and knees (mops were never allowed—down on all fours with a scrub brush was more thorough), she decided to run away.

Little Claire kept near the edge of the playground at every recess for days watching for her chance and at last, just two days before classes were to end, an opportunity arrived. Two boys on the other end of the playground got into a fight, a bad fight, rolling around in the dust, bloodying each other's noses. Both nuns on playground duty, the nun on the boys' side and the one on the girls' side, had to break it up. The boys weren't small and they were very strong and very angry and breaking them up wasn't easy for the old nuns. The fight took all their attention and even the attention of most of the children. Claire simply took a few steps backward, left the playground, and disappeared into the woods.

The nuns had their pets who told on the others and were rewarded for their loyalty, were allowed special privileges and were put in positions of authority as "monitors" or "sergeants at arms" and would have others at their mercy as they were at the mercy of the nuns. She had to be careful of them. Good little Catholic snitches earning points with the sisters and maybe earning points in heaven, who knows. Maybe Claire, when she died, would have to spend some time in purgatory for being such a bad, disobedient little girl, while the sisters' pets

*would be sent straight to heaven. But that time
would pass and then she would be with her mother
for all eternity. Time in purgatory wasn't such a
high price to pay for keeping one's integrity intact
while one lived on this earth. Claire wasn't about to
let the sisters mold her into their image.*

*Claire got away and they couldn't find her.
Though she was just eight years old, she slept in the
woods all alone that night and it was very, very
dark and she was afraid. She slept, nonetheless,
because she was exhausted from running all day.*

*The next day around noon she arrived in her vil-
lage, but she didn't have a home, really. Her mother,
who she always thought of when she thought of
home, was dead so long now Claire couldn't remember her face anymore. Her father, always a heavy
drinker, had given himself over to it after his wife's
death. She found him sitting passed out on the floor,
his back propped up against a wall.*

*Claire went back outside and looked around her
village. No children were there except for the very
young and one crippled boy her age. "Hey, run-
away," the boy called to her. He sat on the little
porch of his wooden house . . . they all had wooden
houses now—playing with his dog. "They were
looking for you. Maybe they're going to put you in
jail now. They told us anybody hiding you would be
put in jail. Why don't you go back to your school?"*

She saw her great-grandmother, her tupiya,
*standing in the doorway of her wooden house. She
ran to her and when she reached her, Ya-ya
embraced her and held her close. "They came to my*

house and looked around," Ya-ya said in Coeur d'Alene Salish. "Of course I don't have any white people's hiding places: no closets, tables, beds. I could tell they were disgusted because I don't have those things. All I have is that big trunk and they opened it and looked all through it. Disturbed my private possessions which I keep in that trunk. The umbilical cords of all my children, some of them long dead now like your grandmother. I hated them for doing that but I didn't let them know. Who knows what they might do to me if they knew? They told that nosey woman next door to tell me they would be back and if I hid you instead of returning you to them they would lock the two of us up. I pretended I didn't understand. You know what? I'm not scared of them. Not scared of their jail either. But I believe they're coming back so let us hurry now! We've got to get ready and get out of here quickly."

Claire

They took the old woman's gentle mare to ride and a small young mule to carry their supplies— their tent and blankets, the kettle and skillet, a little venison jerky. Everything they would need to live in the woods. They rode without a saddle. Claire, always small for her age, was very little at the age of eight. She sat in front of her great-grandmother, who sometimes let her hold the reins. She could remember still how happy she felt when she and her Ya-ya rode out of the village that day, all the neighbors, the nosey woman next door, the crippled boy who wasn't made to attend mission school, even Claire's father, who had staggered outside, all stared at them but said nothing. "Let them tell those men from the government," Ya-ya said in a whisper. "They're too stupid to find us, or too lazy. We'll be safe in the woods for as long as we wish."

The old woman touched Claire's hair now and then and stroked it. Claire knew they couldn't live in the woods forever, but that they could elude the government people for a good long time, and no matter what they did to her for running away, she knew it was the right thing to have done. No matter if they whipped her unconscious or locked her up in a little, dark room like they did to the older children when they were caught swearing (in English, of course) or when they got into fights or when they tried to run away.

Whatever they did to her when they caught her, it was worth it to have this time with her beloved tupiya, this sweet period of freedom. She would remember it always.

They rode for several hours, went down by the eastern shore of the lake and there, near the water, found a good place to camp.

They fished and trapped rabbits and squirrels. They picked huckleberries. Tupiya made bread dough and fried it over their fire in the skillet. They had everything they needed. Life was not hard for the first time in a long while.

At night Ya-ya would tell good stories, though summer was not usually storytelling time. They both knew they probably would not be together when winter came. "Tell me, Ya-ya, tell me about the frog girl who didn't want to marry Coyote. Tell me about the time Coyote pretended he was dying and wanted to apologize to the rabbits for always chasing and killing them. And the time he traded places with the sun and ended up telling everyone's embarrassing secrets, including his own. And the time he decided to get rid of Bear once and for all."

And she would.

They would go for long rides exploring the woods, and Ya-ya would tell her what it was like when she was a little girl Claire's age. She hadn't seen a white person yet at that age, nor had she heard a word of English. They didn't know then what was coming, the wars, and how they would come to be under the rule of the white man and have to do everything the white man wanted.

◄○►
Claire

But Ya-ya didn't mind her wooden house, which was better than the underground winter longhouses by far. Those old longhouses were miserable. Several families living crowded together where it was warm enough to survive but where there was no light except that made by the fire. It smelled bad after a month or so. Sometimes all the members of all the families ended up with lice. Awful. They had to do it because of the harsh winters. But the white man's wooden houses were sturdy and kept out the cold well, and they had windows through which the world outside could be seen. Wood houses, at least in winter, were good, an improvement over the old ways, like many other things the white man brought. Loss of freedom, though, that was no good. People should not have to live this way.

Tupiya's granddaughter was Claire's mother and tupiya told her what her mother was like, as a little girl, as an older girl. She was a beautiful young woman with a mild disposition, not like her own mother, tupiya's eldest daughter, who was ready to do battle over anything, who liked conflict, who liked to argue and get her own way.

Claire's mother had a quiet disposition, a sweet disposition, and was well-loved by everyone who knew her. But her health was always fragile and there were several times, before she was even grown, when she became very ill and nearly died. When she gave birth to Claire, it was the happiest day of her life. She loved her baby very much. She gave her two names, one after a woman who worked at the agency, Claire, a white woman who was both pretty and kind. The white name she would need in this white world they lived in. The other, She-Is-Free, was what she would call her. In the old days, a mother gave her newborn child such a name, She-Smiles, She-Who-Is-Beloved, but this would not be a true name. It expressed the mother's hopes for her child more than anything else. The child would have to earn her true name when she became a woman. "But we don't live that way anymore," Ya-ya said. "Claire" was the only name Claire ever knew.

"Do you believe in Jesus and God, Ya-ya? Do you think they're real?"

"Maybe. Maybe Jesus and God are real. Maybe they are not all that is real, like they say. Maybe they're right. How do we know? Anyway, it doesn't hurt to believe in their Jesus and God. They love humans and want good lives for them on this earth so that they may have good everlasting lives too. It

won't hurt you to go along with their Jesus stories,
will it?"

"No. Only they don't act nice like Jesus told them
they were supposed to."

"They'll be surprised then, when they die, won't
they? Maybe we'll all be surprised when we die."

They knew about the danger. A very little girl
and a very old woman all alone might seem like
easy prey. Sometimes animals were known to attack
and seriously maul humans. But Claire was never
afraid of the animals that lurked in the dark or
maybe lurked in the dark: bears, cougars, wolver-
ines, and the like. And surely there were more of
them back then. But they never saw one dangerous
creature, though they did hear cougars crying in the
night sometimes, and a few times wolves howling.

Claire

"Never mind them. Go back to sleep. They won't
bother us. They're in love. They're not interested in
us. We aren't good-looking young cougaresses are
we? So we've got nothing to worry about."

Coyote's howling didn't bother them, that old
buffoon. They were safe from Coyote as long as they
didn't trust him and allow him to trick them somehow. They heard him often but saw him not once.
He could probably sense they were too smart for
him.

The weather turned cold early that year, before
the end of summer, and Claire and the old woman
weren't able to keep themselves warm enough; they
huddled together under their covers inside their tent
trying to keep warm. Then the rain began, cold, cold
rain drenching them, and there was no way to keep

warm and dry. Tupiya *got sick. She started cough-*
ing and having a hard time of it.

One morning Claire woke up and found tupiya
had picked up their camp and loaded the mule. She
sat on a log beside the fire drinking coffee from a tin
cup. "I think it's time we went back in, don't you?"
Claire nodded. It was. The summer of contentment,
the fine interlude, was over. Knowing it was over
made Claire's throat constrict and ache. She hated
the idea of the good time ending and herself return-
ing to the mission.

She could still remember how sad she felt. She
couldn't stop time.

Back at mission school she wasn't well received. "If
you insist on acting like a little animal, you'll be
treated like one," Sister Bernadette said. They kept a
close eye on her, kept her locked up tight at night, and
she wasn't allowed out on the playground at recess.
Neither was she allowed to go home for visits. She
couldn't be trusted. She didn't return to her village
until she was fourteen and could speak English better
than she could speak her own language. By then, of
course, her tupiya *had died, as she knew she would*
have. Her father, too, had died. She had just one clear
memory of her father: the time she ran away and
found him passed out sitting on the floor propped up
against the wall in their house. She didn't feel sad
that he had died. She felt nothing one way or the
other. She didn't know him. Now she never would.

Claire lay on the big flat warm rock facing the
sun—her long white hair spread out around her
head. She closes her eyes and remembers her

tupiya. Ya-ya and she were fugitives that summer as she was a fugitive now. She drifted off to sleep.

She slept for hours on that rock in the sun and kept on sleeping when the sun went down. When she woke it was the cold that woke her. It was hard finding her clothes in the dark. The moon was not in the proper position to provide much light. As she felt lightly among the bushes for her clothes she hoped she wouldn't stumble and fall in the dark. That wouldn't be a good way for her adventure to end. Finally she found them. The dry clothes smelled fresh and clean like wind and sun and all the other fresh scents of the country, grass and trees and wildflowers. It felt good to put these fresh garments on her body.

She built a little fire and sat near it heating two hotdogs on a stick in the flames. She was hungry, truly hungry, and the hotdogs tasted better than any she could remember. She stayed awake, snug now, fully dressed, covered with the blanket she found in the Oakland bus depot (was it just yesterday?—it seemed like months and months ago) and with the newspaper with the headline about Elizabeth Taylor's divorce over the blanket. Newspapers were good for keeping out cold. She lay awake and enjoyed being free, smelled the smoke from the fire she'd made, looked up at the stars in the sky above. She'd not seen such a sky in a long while and never thought about it. Never realized she'd missed seeing the sky all filled with

◄○►
Claire

stars like this. *Whatever happens now,* she thought, just before closing her eyes and sleeping again, *it's worth it for this.*

Claire spent only two nights camping out alone. Sleeping on the hard ground was really not comfortable for an old person and her bones began to ache; her arthritis acted up.

She woke the first morning with a mild sore throat. By that night it was worse and she had a full-blown head cold. Probably June or someone else on the bus carried the cold germ and gave it to her and she lowered her resistance by camping out in the cold night. Still, it was worth it, worth the delicious taste of freedom.

The second night under the stars she dreamed a destination: she would head for her nephew Joe's house. Joe Whitehawk was a widower with a little boy about Buddy's age. Joe would let her stay as long as she liked. He had her watchdog, Mike, the tough Doberman who had been such a sweet and loving puppy. Sam had trained Mike to be a killer attack dog, to protect his home and the two old people who adopted and loved and took good care of him.

She could help Joe, she thought. He was way off center with his drinking. He was not unlike her own father, a man unable to recover from the death of his young wife, unable to function as he ought. That wasn't good for the boy, Billy. She'd make Joe see, make the boy more comfortable.

She would gently tell Joe he had to pull himself together. She would say to him, "Your son is the motherless child, Joe, not you. He looks to you for strength, to love him and make him feel safe in this world. How can you make anyone safe when you're drunk?" Maybe she could get Joe to take them all camping down by the lake before this summer ended. She would love to do that. Maybe she would tell that boy some Indian stories. She wondered if Joe had told him any.

She walked back to the little place, Biggs Junction (you couldn't call it a town), where the bus depot and convenience store were and she went to the cafe for a meal. Trucks, great big trucks, were parked in front. Inside she sat at the counter and had a bowl of stew and a cup of coffee and then used the men's room. Actually, there were no women here, except for the waitresses. On her way out, a truck driver who wasn't looking where he was going, talking to his friends over his shoulder as he was leaving, bumped into her and knocked her to the floor.

"Oh, Christ! I'm sorry, mister. Are you okay?" She broke her fall with her hands, landing in a sitting position. The green and yellow baseball cap fell from her head and her long braids tumbled down. She put the cap back on but let the braids stay free. She was nearer Indian country now where you would find a man with long braids, an Indian man, and it was not a strange sight. The trucker held out a hand and she took it and he pulled her to her feet. "Are you all right? Are you sure?" Concerned because of her age. When an old person takes a fall it can be very serious. Claire nodded she was all right. "I could take you to the emergency hospital ten miles down the road if you want. Let's do that. Let them have a look at you."

"I'm not hurt." The cold she had naturally made her voice deeper, a most convincing man's voice. "But I could use a ride. Where you headed?" Spokane, he said.

Spokane! That was close, just sixty miles from the northern border of the reservation. "Can you give me a lift?" So it was that Claire rode in a semi all the way from a little truck stop in Oregon to Spokane, Washington. And there she found the Greyhound Depot again and had enough money to buy a ticket to Coeur d'Alene. From there she decided she would hitchhike to the reservation.

She would ask Joe to hide her since she was a fugitive, and Joe would say, "Of course, Auntie. Stay as long as you like." And she would stay with them and maybe she would help Joe turn himself around. She was strong of mind and body, even though she was almost an octogenarian, and still able. She would keep house for them and cook. Pick wild berries and put them up for winter. She'd give the little boy the attention he needed. She would go to them, her nephew and his little boy, and there she'd be welcome and useful. And she would thank God each day she was no longer an unwelcome guest in her daughter-in-law's house and no longer an inmate of Loma Vista.

By the time she boarded the bus to Coeur d'Alene, Claire felt sick for real. Weak. Her throat was so sore it hurt to breathe, and her chest was all congested. But she would be all right once she got to Joe's house and got some rest. Inside the crowded bus it seemed very, very warm to her. Once she was seated she took a good look around. Nobody else seemed uncomfortable. Nobody but her took their jackets off. She leaned her cheek against the green-tinted glass window. It felt so cool, so blessedly cool. The whole world outside looked green now, a sick-looking green like bile a person with an empty stomach throws up when he vomits.

◄○►
Claire

The bus driver announced through a microphone that this coach would stop in Coeur d'Alene and then would be continuing on to Bonner's Ferry. *"Continuing on,"* she thought. *"Shouldn't say that. 'Continuing to Bonner's Ferry' or 'Going on to Bonner's Ferry.'"* The nuns pounded correct grammar into her head so hard it stayed there. How funny that Indians, at least those of her generation who were forced to attend mission school, spoke better English than most white people did. Continuing on. It bugged her.

Claire closed her eyes and saw her beloved husband's face. *"Sam."* *He smiled, his face lit by the sun. "What happens when we die, Sam?" Could be anything. Could be like the Hindus think and we build up karma, good or bad, and get reborn as a queen or a hyena or something according to what*

kind of life you earned. Could be you turn into a
ghost of some kind. That's a possibility.

Catholics, who don't allow divorce, or do but
no remarriage, think you're completely changed
in heaven. You're a completely different form
concerned with only spiritual things. Nobody
cares about husbands or wives or sweethearts
anymore. Everyone is all the same. All without
gender. Wouldn't homosexuals be the same, too,
then? One of her sons was a homosexual, she
thought. Either he was a homosexual or a middle-aged man who happened never to have married but had lived with a close male friend for the
past fifteen years.

There's no reason why this son, Ernie, should
be shut out of heaven. Especially not the Catholic
heaven. Except Ernie was not such a good son. He
didn't even make the effort like Ozzie did. He visited her for two hours at Loma Vista last
Christmas and on Mother's Day he sent a floral
arrangement. A lot of the inmates received floral
arrangements on Mother's Day and Father's Day
instead of visits. Maybe Ernie wouldn't be let right
in to Catholic heaven because there he was just
across the bay in San Francisco and never phoned
his Mom, never tried to see to her needs. Well,
Ernie was the youngest of her three boys. Nothing
much was ever expected of him as such. Ernie was
a bit spoiled. She hoped he wouldn't have to do
time in purgatory for being an inattentive son.

Once Mormon missionaries came out to the
house and started telling Claire and Sam about

the Mormon religion, all their beliefs and whatnot. It was interesting and those two boys, the
missionaries, were really nice, very polite. Of
course they weren't going to convert, but those
boys were so pleasant and she enjoyed their
spiel, even though one of the things they said
about Indians was silly, she thought.

They thought Indians and all dark-skinned
people (except for Negroes who were descended
from Cain) used to be white but then their ances-
tor, Laman, committed a terrible sin so God
made him turn brown. And He told Laman that
from then on all his descendants would be
brown, but one day they would make it up to
God and he would forgive them and they would
all turn white again. Something like that.

Claire

One thing, though, she wished were true that
the Mormons had told her about heaven was that
everyone in the hereafter would be restored to
their prime, that mothers and fathers and children and husbands and wives, all the dearly
departed, would find each other again and all be
happy. Husbands and wives would have sexual
relations in this Mormon heaven and even, if
they wished, have spiritual children. She hoped
this were true, that she would be young and
beautiful once again and she and Sam would be
together, have sex with each other the way they
used to. That would be so lovely. She wondered if
in Mormon Heaven, since they were Mormons
and it *was* their heaven, did they practice
polygamy?

She thought not. Polygamy used to exist, it seemed, in societies in which there was a surplus of single women due to war or whatever and widows and sometimes orphaned children weren't up to taking care of themselves. Then some man, especially if he were wealthy, would marry more than one woman and provide for all his wives. In heaven, all the kinds of heaven, everyone would have enough. No one would have to compromise themselves in any way. And she was sure her Sam would have no interest in taking another wife, even if it were allowed.

But Sam was not her first husband. Her first husband, whom she'd married when she was seventeen, was George, Sam's brother. George joined the army and was sent over to France. Claire, who was pregnant with Ozzie, stayed with his parents. Sam tried to join the army too but he had a heart murmur that kept him out. George was killed in the war shortly after Ozzie was born. He never knew he had a son. They sent his body home and gave him a military funeral, draped his coffin with the Star-Spangled Banner, which had only forty-eight stars back then, and folded it in the correct way and gave it to Claire. George was just twenty when he died. Hardly more than a boy.

Claire was sorry her young husband died, but, she was ashamed to admit to herself, she liked Sam more than she had ever liked his brother. Sam married his brother's widow as old-time Indians used to do, because she and her child needed a husband and father to look after them. But Sam told her, not right away, after they were married five years, that he loved her all along, began loving her the minute he laid eyes on her when George brought her home to have dinner with his family, when Claire was just fifteen and recently released from mission school.

Claire lived with a white family in town looking after their children, helping with the housework. That's how she supported herself. She was glad to marry George and begin her own family. She didn't think much of being a household servant, though it beat both mission school and Loma Vista.

━◄○►━
Claire

But what would she do if heaven was like the Mormons said and she'd get there and there she'd be with two husbands? Probably that sort of thing wouldn't bother Mormons. But Claire didn't want two husbands. What would they do? She would choose Sam, of course. Would George's feelings be hurt? Would he have to be alone then for all eternity? Probably not. Most likely he'd met some nice single woman and they had gotten together and married in heaven.

And then there was Clairice, their only daughter, who died when she was a baby. If her daughter had lived, Claire wouldn't have been sent to Loma Vista. Daughters don't allow their mothers to be put out and not many sons-in-law would make the demands as daughters-in-law were known to do. According to Mormon belief, in heaven little Clairice would grow to adulthood, to her prime. It would be good, Claire thought, if she and Sam and baby Clairice could all be together and they could raise her and watch her grow. Who knows what it might be like.

Well, she was going to be eighty years old at the end of summer. She would probably find out soon enough. Or maybe she wouldn't. Maybe it would be nothing. The great darkness and only that and their whole lives, and everyone's, would be like drops of water going over Niagara Falls. And their little human lives would really mean only what they made them mean.

She fell asleep and dreamed of Sam, not the young man in his prime, but the old man she buried nearly four years ago. She saw Sam's face in her dream and heard him say, *"Hurry, dear. I'm waiting."* And then his image faded and she surfaced from her deep sleep, her face pressed against the cold, green-tinted glass. She was in Coeur d'Alene, Idaho.

She got off the bus, a little old lady dressed like a man, and walked out to Highway-95 carrying her plaid blanket, feeling miserable with her cold and sore throat, and she stuck out her thumb. Almost right away a young man in a pickup truck, who was going to Moscow, far south of the reservation, stopped for her.

"You shouldn't be hitchhiking, sir," the young man said, "it's very dangerous. A woman's body was found in the woods just out of Coeur d'Alene last week. Nobody knows what happened, but she was known to hitchhike." Claire nodded and said she knew he was right and she would never hitch a ride again. She hoped she'd never have to.

The young man, who was white, worked for a logging company up north. He worked many hours and there was never enough time. He hoped Claire wouldn't mind that he was going to drive very, very fast, but he was a good driver. He was going to see his girlfriend, who was a student at the university in Moscow. He missed her so much. He just had to see her. But he had to drive back to the camp that very night and he had to get some sleep because he had to be up by five A.M. the next morning. "You don't look so good," he said. "Are you sick? Are you going home now?"

◄O►
Claire

"I'm going to my nephew's house now. I am sick but I'm going to be okay. My nephew will take care of me, take me in to see the doctor if I don't get well after a good night's sleep."

The young man left her at the mailbox at the end of Joe's long drive. "You take it easy now, Pops," he said, and she answered he'd better take his driving easy or he would never see his girlfriend. He grinned. She stepped down out of the cab and he pulled the door closed. They waved to each other and there she was. Almost home.

Joe's little house, at the end of the mile-long drive, was nestled close to a group of pine forested hills. Between the highway and the house, on both sides of the drive as far as one could see, were wheat fields, oceans of ripe yellow wheat. Smoke rose out of the chimney. Joe's pickup, the same one he'd had when she last saw him, sat in front of the house. She started walking down the road. Claire felt tired, very, very tired. Too tired to want to eat. Too tired to want anything except to lie in a warm, comfortable bed and sleep and sleep and sleep.

Joe, who had just returned from driving Billy to school, stood at the kitchen sink washing dishes. The dogs, the little terrier who had wandered onto the place a few months ago and never left, the arthritic old Lab, and Mike, the Doberman his aunt had given him, alerted him that someone was coming down the road. He picked up his binoculars, which he kept on the windowsill above the sink, because from this location he could see all of the road clearly.

A small, old Indian man with long braids walked down the road towards the house, not at all daunted, it seemed, by the dogs. He'd better go out there and see who it was, keep the dogs from attacking the old fellow. He put on his coat and went out the door, crossed the log bridge over the creek. "Quiet down, you guys. Knock it off. Mike. Theodore. Bennie. Knock it off," he shouted. The dogs knocked it off, for the most part. The old man waved to Joe and Joe waved back, though he didn't recognize him. He was sure the old man was somebody he knew. He did look familiar.

Then the old man took his baseball cap off his head and waved it in the clean, crisp morning air and called out in Coeur d'Alene Salish: "Mike! Mike! *Whui'nech nep I ill ish uss. Ah, Dune.*"* Mike whimpered and then took off running as fast as he could. When Mike reached the old man, the man bent down and hugged Mike around the neck and that fierce, always aloof watchdog licked the old, smiling face.

◄O►
Claire

* Mike! Mike! Come here, boy. Come greet your mom.

Dora Lee in Love

One beautiful morning in late summer, Dora Lee walked along the beach enjoying the fresh sea air, the sun sparkling on the water, the deep, warm blue of the sky.

Suddenly she came upon the body of a man lying on the beach all wrapped in long, tangled seaweed tentacles. Gift wrapped it seemed, just then washed ashore, she guessed. A few little fish, caught in the vegetation, flipped about wildly. His clothes, a red and black checkered flannel shirt, blue jeans, and red suspenders, were soaking wet and his black hair plastered itself to his forehead and face.

"A dead body," she thought. "A dead body?" It didn't look dead though. "What do I do now? Call the Coast Guard. But what if he washes back to sea while I'm gone? Better pull him away from the water where no waves can reach him." But, as she considered what to do, the body, very much alive, let out a long, loud snore.

Now she *really* didn't know what to do. He drew in a long breath and held it longer than seemed humanly possible before letting out another long, loud snore.

Dora Lee knelt in the sand and pulled the seaweed that wrapped around the man loose until she managed to free the four fish. They no longer flipped wildly about since they were almost out of breath, but they gasped and writhed just a little, their sleek, silvery bodies caked with dry sand. Dora Lee picked them up one by one and threw them back into the sea. She looked at the man lying at her feet and thought (though not seriously), "Maybe I should throw him back, too."

In the years to come she would remember that moment and that fleeting thought—"throw him back, too." How easy it would have been to just drag him far enough so that the waves could not wash him back out again, then go home and call the Coast Guard or the police or some other authority and tell them there's an unconscious man lying on the beach. Or to have just stepped over him and gone on her way. But she felt her destiny, and who was she to resist destiny?

The man was not a pretty sight. He reeked of, besides the smells of the sea, something alcoholic. Something that reminds one of the smell of blueberries. Probably he fell out of a boat somewhere not far from shore. Or maybe someone who wanted him dead got him drunk and threw him into the ocean. Or maybe he'd washed ashore someplace else last night but hadn't come to and the waves came and carried him back into the sea and shortly after washed him ashore again, this time on Dora Lee's beach.

Dora Lee, who was very strong in her youth, disentangled and then lifted him, her arms under his arms, hands clasped together in front of his chest, and, walking backwards, dragged him down the beach until her house was in sight.

Two teenage boys and a dog walked towards her in the damp, firm sand barefoot. They kept throwing a stick for the dog to go fetch, sometimes throwing it out so far the dog would have to swim out to get it. She knew these boys. The mother of one worked as a waitress down at the cafe.

"Hi, Dora," one of them said. "What you got there?"

"I found this guy washed ashore."

"Gonna keep him, then, eh?"

"I don't know. We'll see."

"Need some help? Let us give you a hand."

"Okay. Good. Thank you."

One of the boys lifted him by his feet, the other by his arms, and they carried him all the way down to Dora Lee's house. There they stopped and rested a moment.

"Man!" one of the boys said. "This guy weighs a lot for such a little squirt." Carrying him up the long flight of outdoor steps was trickier and took some time. They about dropped him several times and had to stop.

Dora Lee had gone ahead and opened the door. She'd put a pillow on the sofa, and when they carried her man inside, she told them to deposit him there. Then she covered him with a blanket from her own bed.

"Thank you very much, boys. Getting him up here by myself would have been hard. Thank you." She gave them each a bottle of Coke, which they seemed happy to have.

When the boys left, she uncovered the snoring, passed-out or sleeping man, and took his wet clothes off of him. She wanted, very much, to see what the man's face looked like under that three or four days' growth of stubble. Dora Lee lathered up the passed-out man's face and shaved it clean except for the little mustache, which she left as it was. She did nick him, but just once, just a little nick. He didn't wake. Then she combed his freshly shampooed hair back, and though she thought he badly needed a haircut, she resisted the urge, as she resisted the urge to give him a manicure. Then she stood up, stepped back, and admired her handiwork. His age was hard to tell, but he had no grey hair and his brown skin was smooth. She guessed he had to be young or early middle-aged (he would tell her when he woke he was twenty-nine, a little younger than herself). A little round man with a round face. Not at all unpleasant looking. Not bad. Not half-bad.

He slept all day and into the night. Dora Lee made some clam chowder with clams she'd dug herself. She knew he'd be hungry when he came to. Then she sat in a rocking chair beside the sofa and read a few pages of a book she'd borrowed from the library that was about the life of the famous psychic Edgar Cayce. She dozed off.

"Your name must be angel," he said, rousing her from her sleep. She opened her eyes. Her found man, who was stark naked, knelt beside her. His eyes, large, so dark a shade of brown as to appear black, fringed with long black eyelashes, were the most beautiful she'd ever seen.

"You look like an angel," he said. *He needs glasses,* she thought. His voice was deep, rich, the voice of a radio announcer. "I'm going to call you Angel," he said. "Did you save me, Angel?" She nodded. "Did you dive off the boat and rescue me?" She shook her head no. She sure didn't and she wouldn't have either had she been there. She did not swim.

He remembered drinking in a bar near the ferry landing on the mainland. When the bartender refused to serve him any more drinks, he went outside and got in his car and drove to where cars had begun to line up. He parked his car in line behind a brown pickup truck with American plates that had a bumper sticker that said: "You Want It? Get It Like I Did! Work For It!" He remembered thinking it amusing. The truck owner must have a very high opinion of his vehicle, imagining other drivers coveted it. He took his whiskey flask from the glove compartment and continued to drink. On board the ferry he began feeling sick and ran out to the deck. The last thing he remembered was hanging his head over the side of the boat and vomiting. Sick as a damned dog! He was going to stop drinking. That was all there was to it.

"I found you on the beach. You're on Vancouver Island. Washed ashore."

"Thank you. Thank you from the bottom of my heart. Thank you for bringing me to your home." The squatting man took Dora Lee's hand and raised it to his lips and kissed it.

"Are you married, Angel? Will you marry me? I know I probably don't look it sitting here naked like this, but I'm a rich man. I can take care of you. You'll never want for anything again." Dora Lee, in spite of herself, was charmed. That night was the first night they made love. It was the first time Dora Lee ever made love. His name was Jean-Paul and she was amazed to find, weeks later, after he'd fully recovered, that he had spoken the truth: he was indeed a rich man. He had never held a job of any kind. His parents had owned land, lots of it, and when they died and left everything to Jean-Paul when he was just nineteen, he invested in more real estate and began to play the stock market, which he no longer did. He lived in his family's fine big house on the beach at White Rock, which was a small resort city right on the U.S.-Canada border. He owned a lot of beach-front property there. White people took out hundred-year leases and built expensive houses on Jean-Paul's property and paid him very well. Jean-Paul owned some timberland, too. He'd not sold any timber in a long while because the price was so low. He would just hang on to it until lumber prices went up again. One of his cars, his main car, was a banana-yellow Jaguar. Jean-Paul was not well-educated or well-bred. He was, however, *rich*. Dora Lee was in love and it wouldn't have mattered to her were he poor. She would have continued to work at the cafe and supported him if need be. Even though she would have loved him poor, would have loved him no matter what, his wealth absolutely thrilled her.

Jean-Paul and Dora Lee took a cruise to Puerto Vallarta. At sea they stood in the moonlight looking at the water and sky. Dora Lee wore an expensive red shawl of hand-woven wool and had just had her hair cut and styled that day at the ship's salon. "Do you like it, Jean-Paul?" she'd asked. He'd said he loved her long hair. Most women, he'd said, overdo the makeup and perm stuff. Natural is better. Now, when she timidly asked if he liked her new, very short, stylish haircut, he said, "It makes you look eighteen!" and took her in his arms, drew her close, and kissed her. She *felt* eighteen. That very night, after they'd made love several times and dawn was about to break, Jean-Paul proposed: "Dora Lee, my angel, will you marry me?" "Of course I will," she answered, "of course I will." Jean-Paul took the diamond ring from his coat pocket and slipped it on her finger. Even in the pale moonlight it sparkled.

They married in Puerto Vallarta and stayed there two weeks, letting their ship sail without them. Dora Lee, who never cared to drink, drank champagne and got a little drunk not one night but two. They made love standing on the balcony of their hotel room and one night in the life guard's chair on the beach. They danced. They swam. They made a lot of love. When the time came to leave, they flew back to British Columbia first class. *There I was*, she thought, *a poor, lonely short-order cook who had never had a date in my life, and now here I am, a happily married woman no longer alone and no longer poor.* The first three or four months of their marriage was, at least to Dora Lee, an enchanted time of sheer bliss. Then, one afternoon Jean-Paul went into their bedroom and a few minutes later called to his wife.

"Dora Lee! Dora Lee! Get your fat butt in here! What is *that*?!*" He was pointing at a large tumbler with a little water in it on the floor beside the bed. Jean-Paul had made himself some iced tea the night before and sipped it while he lay watching TV. The glass was where he had left it. What enraged him was that it was still there.

"Why didn't you pick that glass up, carry it into the kitchen, and wash it, Dora Lee? Do you think you're too good to wash dishes, is that it? You're my wife, Dora Lee, and," Jean-Paul, for emphasis, kicked the glass against the woodwork breaking it into a thousand pieces, "a wife, in case you don't know it, Miss High-and-Mighty, is *supposed* to keep house! Get your lazy fat butt into gear and clean up this mess!"

With him standing over her, arms crossed in front of his chest, she cleaned it up, working slowly so as not to cut her fingers on the shards of broken glass. She was utterly bewildered. This was not the gentle man she knew. Maybe, she hoped, this was a freak thing, the likes of which would never happen again.

But Jean-Paul had shown his true colors and would never again pretend to be the man she fell in love with, the one who sang love songs to her, told her stories and jokes, was always happy. From then on Dora Lee came to know the mean, violent, crazy Jean-Paul. Dora Lee, when she was in love, imagined God had washed Jean-Paul ashore that fateful day, that he was God's gift to her. In time though, she came to believe he had been put before her not by God but by Lucifer himself.

Women on the Run

B*obbi: Detroit is like Memphis, Milwaukee, Pittsburgh, Corpus Christi, New Orleans. The places I've been my five long years on the run are all alike. I hitched a ride in . . . I forget. Eight hours' driving time away. It doesn't matter where it was or where I am. Not much. Damned cold in Detroit. And the snow doesn't seem likely to stop anytime soon.*

I don't have a winter coat. Someone stole it from me in the fall, broke into my flea-bag hotel room, took my watch, too. I do have a pair of sturdy work shoes with thick soles. I'll get by. Going to find an Indian bar. Have a drink and a little something to eat. I don't want to be alone when the clock strikes midnight 1988.

"Sister, can you spare a dollar? I haven't eaten in three days," an Indian wino in a long, black overcoat says, trying to make a pitiful-looking face. He's appeared from out of the shadows. He holds out three fingers and repeats, "Three days." Yeah sure. Because you've been too busy drinking to think about eating. I can spare nothin', but I reach into my jeans' pocket and find a quarter, a dime, and a nickel and give them to him. He smiles and thanks me. "Happy New Year, Sister."

"Happy New Year yourself, Mister."
The snow keeps falling.

Lena Bowman's Journal: January 11, 1988, Vancouver, British Columbia

I write a little every day in accordance with my New Year's resolution. This is not as easy as I thought it would be when I made that resolution. It is a discipline I must practice.

I am a writer who has not written for over a year. I am desperate to write. I thought the mere physical act of sitting down at my writing table and committing words to paper would do the trick—the way you could get old cars to start, sometimes, by pushing them as fast as you could until the engine finally turned over. And sometimes therapists will manually move a person's paralyzed limbs in an effort to get them working again.

I've read self-help books that advise depressed people to carry on and go through the motions, "act as if" everything were normal. I know from experience that this is effective. Instead of lying in bed all day not eating, feeling terrible, you get up and take a shower and put on clean, pressed clothes. Fix your hair, do your makeup. Go to work. Go shopping. Come home. Do your laundry. Make yourself a nice meal. Feel terrible if you can't feel any other way, feel as though life is meaningless. Ignore the bleak emotions. Ignore the desolation of your inner landscape.

Keep acting as if you are not depressed, as if you are fine. If someone asks, "How are you?" don't tell. Reply, "Fine," and lo and behold, one day you really are fine. You will love life again.

That is what I'm doing when I force myself to write. I'm writing as if I *can*. One day I hope I will.

It's a tedious undertaking. But I have started a novel. No, I haven't exactly *started*. I have come up with an idea for a novel and am now planning it.

It's about a woman, Helen, who is sort of like myself, whose third husband—the third man to take a public vow to love her for richer or poorer, in sickness and in health, until death do they part—leaves her for another woman (if you could call her a woman)—the next door neighbor's baby-sitter. Eighteen, but not the mature eighteen I was. A young, childlike eighteen. Which is, I suppose, part of her appeal. She is also beautiful.

Helen, my protagonist, was orphaned at an early age and her three grown sisters, who had big families of their own, resented being stuck with a child sister. They take turns raising her, but none of them wants her. She works hard trying to get them to like her. She does a lot of baby-sitting, a lot of diaper washing. She does anything they ask from washing dishes to bathing babies to mowing lawns. Once in a great while her sisters are friendly and kind. She lives for those moments. She desperately wants their approval.

More often they go out of their way to be mean. One day when she is thirteen she sits at her brother-in-law's desk, which was in the corner of the living room, but separated from it by a long, high bookcase. Helen writes poetry to express her feelings and to keep herself company. She leaves her pen and about ten sheets of notebook paper on the top of the desk while she goes into the adjoining kitchen to get a glass of water. The sister whose house it is happens to walk past the little study area just then and sees the ten sheets of paper, five of them with poetry written on them. She yells, "Who left this mess here?" and grabs the pages before Helen can rescue them. Her big sister wads them up, yelling, "There's too many of us for anyone to leave messes like this lying around." Helen is unable to wrest the wadded up pages from her sister's hand before she stuffs them in the trash.

Helen always feels like an outsider. By the time she turns sixteen she can no longer remember her parents' faces or voices.

At sixteen she marries a boy she meets at a gas station where he works as an attendant. He graduated from high school the year before and has saved enough money to begin college. Helen and her first husband live in the University of Washington's married student housing. Helen, who took secretarial courses when she was in school, gets a job as a clerk typist. Her husband, who is on his way to law school, studies very hard. Helen gets a night job at a doughnut shop. Though very young and strong, she sometimes gets very, very tired. Her

feet ache when she gets off work at the doughnut shop. Her head aches by the end of the
workday at the office.

She tells herself it will all be worthwhile when
he finally becomes a lawyer. They will come up
in the world then. Her husband has a motorcycle
but no car. They could buy a nice car. They could
buy a house. They could take a vacation. Maybe
Helen could quit work and go to college herself.
Or, maybe they could start a family of their own.

At the end of four years, on the day after his
college graduation (he had been accepted at law
school), he tells Helen he has outgrown her. His
new wife-to-be is already in law school. Her
father is an important criminal attorney. Helen's
husband and his new wife will be lawyers
together. They are "intellectual equals," Helen's
husband tells her.

He wishes Helen well. "Have a good life," he
says as he walks out the door for the last time.

Helen has been studying, too. She has learned
how to write term papers by typing her husband's for him. She takes the SAT and even
though she has just an eighth grade education,
she scores in the top ten percent and is accepted
at the University of Washington (or "U Dub" as
it is affectionately known). She graduates college
and then earns an MSW.

Helen thinks she can make a substantial con-
tribution to society as a social worker. Now, she
thinks, instead of typing, filing, and serving
doughnuts and coffee, she will better the world by

helping the needy. She soon becomes very disillusioned. When she works for the welfare department she encounters mainly single mothers. Some of them are third- and fourth-generation recipients. Others are just poor and have shabby clothes and live in low-rent dumps and can't get hold of enough money to get on their feet. For all of them, welfare is a trap.

When she works for child protective services, most of her work involves investigating reports that a woman's husband or boyfriend is sexually molesting her children. Once a woman calls to report her friend, who is a welfare recipient. The friend is also disabled, but the woman is sure she is on welfare because her friend often speaks of her caseworker's visits. The friend's live-in boyfriend had held her two-year-old's fingers over the gas flame to "teach him a lesson," because he is always getting up before the adults and turning on the gas burners, which is dangerous. The child has been scolded and spanked and just can't seem to learn. The caller did not witness her friend's boyfriend holding the little toddler's fingers over the flames. Her friend had told her and she'd seen the child's burned hands. She gives the friend's maiden name and the other name, and the father of one of her children's names, which she sometimes uses. The caller gives the telephone number and address. Yet no one can find any of the disabled welfare mother's names on the welfare roles. So there is no investigation. But people who work at little odd jobs to supplement their meager income, baby-sit, or take in sewing because they need to buy a fridge or get phone service, are regularly busted. Social work is soon just a job. And a poorly paying one at that. A job without a future. Helen changes jobs regularly. They are all bad.

Years later, when she is about to turn forty, her third husband, like his predecessors, dumps her for someone "better." She slashes her wrists but her neighbor finds her and calls an ambulance.

After they give her a transfusion and sew up her wrists she has to stay at the psych ward for a time. There she comes to understand that deep down she believes her husbands have left her because she is a defective person unworthy of love. She isn't good enough, and she will never be good enough. What is wrong with her is something intrinsic. She can't change. She has had three husbands who left her. She will never find a husband she can plan a future with, because sooner or later he would find someone better. She will be alone forever. There is no way she can change who she is.

She learns in the psych ward she suffers from low self-esteem and has to listen to her inner voice when it says things like, "You stupid bitch!" "You fuck-up! No wonder nobody wants you!" "You're getting older and uglier all the time." "Your life has always been shit and will always be shit as long as you live." And the right way to answer back is with affirmative things like, "I am not stupid. I am not worthless. I am a good person." She thinks she needs more than this. More than just answering herself. While in the psych ward she reads a self-help book that says to imagine herself as she was at five or six years old (she was five when her parents died in an auto accident). One's inner child, frightened and alone, still lives inside a person's psyche. The simplistic book says to talk to your inner child. Say reassuring things to the little kid. Say things like, "I'm here, Honey. I am a strong capable adult and I love you. I'll take care of you. There's nothing to be afraid of. Nothing." And to take yourself on your lap and give yourself a big hug.

After she is released, Helen runs into one of the three sisters who raised her and one of her teenage daughters in a supermarket. They obviously see her but ignore her. She feels ashamed and blushes. But this time she realizes that she has nothing to be ashamed of, that there is really nothing wrong with her. There's something wrong with her sisters and their families. They are the ones who are small and meanspirited. They treated her like a dog whom they would throw a bone to once in awhile. And she is behaving like a dog whose master kicks it. The next time she sees the abusive master, she comes running up to him hoping for some kind of recognition, pat on the head, or a kind word. She has to hurry out of the store without doing her shopping. She feels humiliated. She sits in her car and weeps until all the shame, anxiety, tension, and anger are depleted. She sees her sister and niece leave the store carrying their groceries, get into their car, and drive away.

She decides to run away from Seattle and everything she knows. Make a clean break from her past and all that will remind her of it. Seattle, lovely though it is, is full of ghosts. She wants to go to a place where she will have to run into neither relatives nor exes, will never have to even hear anything about them. Indian communities are always so small and inbred. Everyone knows everyone else's business. The Seattle Indian community has a saying regarding this: "Everyone knows everything you do before you do it." She wants to make a fresh start somewhere, but she doesn't want to leave the Pacific Northwest.

She runs to the city she believes is the most beautiful city in the world: Vancouver, B.C. And here she finds she can breathe freely.

Reviewers said my last novel was "autobiographical" and my characters "thinly disguised" fictional versions of myself. The main character of my last novel is a 100-year-old Eskimo woman telling an anthropologist her great love story. Her love was an Indian man whom she met at a government boarding school they were forced to attend. She and the anthro sit in an igloo near a warm fire. She smokes a pipe. She has no teeth and her skin is all wrinkled up. So *she* is supposedly a disguised version of me, eh? I wonder what they'll say about this one.

Once I took a writing workshop with the novelist and critic Diane Johnson. Diane said one should ignore what critics say and be glad they say anything at all. Even if your work is misunderstood and negatively reviewed, the important thing is getting your name and the name of your book in print, and getting the public to know that you and your work exist. But don't read the reviews yourself. Diane stopped reading reviews after one began: "This is obviously the work of a sick and twisted mind."

When I was an overworked, disillusioned social worker who believed literature called her (but I was too busy to write), I wanted to answer my calling. I believed my destiny was to write. I worked all day at my office job, then, for four hours every night, instead of working at a doughnut shop, I wrote a novel. It only took five months.

A major publisher brought it out and it was well-received. My second novel established me. I was now a writer. I quit my day job at the home for unwed mothers. I began my career as a full-time writer. So far, I've made about the same annually as I used to make as a secretary.

I keep afloat writing magazine articles. Sometimes I am invited to speak at a university. I was Distinguished Visiting Writer one year at "U Dub," and I was Writer-in-Residence for one semester at the University of Oregon in Eugene. I received a creative writing fellowship from the National Endowment for the Arts a couple of years ago but have been turned down four times by Guggenheim. One of my novels, the third, was a huge critical success and won a number of awards and a faithful but small following. It went out of print after just one year.

I submitted three short stories and a synopsis for a collection of short fiction to Random House. It was turned down. Only really famous people, they told me, like, say, Raymond Carver, Joyce Carol Oates, or Stephen King can expect to make a profit on a short story collection. I was just an obscure writer. Nobody would be interested in my collection. I'd have to write another novel and it had better be more ambitious and more successful than the last. One can't build a literary career by taking a step down. I didn't know I was obscure. That last book was nominated for the Pulitzer Prize (but was not a finalist). What can I do to save myself? And what about the calling? What about that? At its best, writing *is* a spiritual practice. Please don't let me see writing as a dead-end the way I came to see social work. I underwent a crisis of faith, like a priest who doubts the existence of God.

Then the trouble began with Jeremy. He started going out and staying out all night. Sometimes the phone would ring and the caller would hang up when I answered. I knew the signs. He found fault with me. He said I was lazy. Why didn't I get a job? When I reminded him I was a writer and didn't work for anyone else, he reminded me that I finished my last book more than a year before. "So how does that make you a writer now?" he asked. "Look at you. You're no writer! And when you do write, your novels are

God-awful. No one with half a brain is interested in reading them. And what's more, you know it! You know you're good for nothing." Yes, I knew it. Useless. Good for nothing. I was just making a fool of myself trying to be a writer. Of course, Jeremy was trying to justify his intentions to divorce me for another woman. I heard his little Lolita is working at Kentucky Fried Chicken to help support him these days. I'm glad I'm not her.

I never wrote a line from that day when Jeremy told me off until New Year's Day when I forced myself to pick up the pen.

If I am not a writer, what am I? An unemployed bum who has stranded herself in a foreign country where she cannot legally work? Just a depressed, desperate, middle-aged woman trying not to answer a calling but to justify her existence and give herself an identity? I have to write. It's a matter of survival. Write. Write. Write. One word at a time.

I worked until around noon when I gave up for the day, made myself a tuna sandwich and got a diet pop from the fridge, switched on the TV, and plopped myself down.

The noon news was on.

"Early this morning," the newscaster said, "the Royal Canadian Mounted Police, acting on a tip, arrested American Indian fugitive Roberta Trumaine in Windsor, Ontario. Trumaine jumped a one million dollar bail in Seattle in 1983. Trumaine was charged with eight counts of racketeering, one charge of receiving stolen goods, and the attempted murder of her now ex-husband's mistress, Leona Garr.

"An interesting footnote: when Trumaine jumped bail, she weighed in at more than three hundred pounds. At the time of her arrest this morning, she weighed a svelte one hundred and forty-five pounds." Then the newscaster turned to his colleague who sat near him at a counter. "Think of that, Gloria! She's down to less than half her former weight! Wish I knew her secret!" He patted his paunch.

"That's what a life on the run can do, eh? There must be an easier way. At any rate, I imagine that immense weight loss made quite an effective disguise." Ted nodded in agreement.

"In other news today, former first lady Margaret Trudeau . . ." I switched off the set.

I know Roberta Trumaine! Bobbi T.

When I was a little girl I used to play with her kids, Claudine and Wes Jr. She was the wife of a fisherman back then. She lived near my oldest sister. Bobbi and her husband and two kids all lived in a little two-room shack. Then later, after she and Wes broke up, Bobbi T. became the fisher for the family. Her mother lived with them then. Bobbi T. was the only commercial Indian fisher-*woman* at the time. They called her "Lucky Lady." She did well, much better than her first husband ever did.

Bobbi T. married a very handsome man after she started getting prosperous. A handsome, useless man who gambled a lot, they said, and was always employed by Bobbi. She ended up divorcing him and having to pay him a big settlement not unlike the rich, glamorous older movie stars do when their marriages to handsome, poor, much younger men come to an end.

Bobbi became enormously successful. She owned a fleet of fishing boats in Seattle and a resort in Arizona and God knows what all. She was very, *very* rich.

The news about Bobbi T. perked me up. More. *Excited* me. I saw possibilitie$. Here she was this famous (or *infamous*) fugitive and I knew her all of my life. Sort of. I grew up in the same community she lived in, where she was once poor like all the rest, but then, instead of moving someplace like Beverly Hills, she stayed right there among her own people, who remained poor, and she flaunted her wealth, kept a high profile. Her ex-husband, Wes, was my brother-in-law's first cousin.

Maybe a publisher would consider that enough of an in to give me a contract (and a good-sized advance) to write a book about Bobbi.

Bobbi T. had been charged with many things, among them hiring a hit man to kill Wes' former lover, Leona Garr. That was a long time ago when Bobbi T. was merely rich for an Indian, not *really* rich.

Bobbi's first business was a little tavern, the Sasquatch, which did quite well. She made her first *big* money when she opened a gambling casino on the Indian land she'd inherited. It was just two double-wide trailers featuring twenty-one and poker and some Chinese game and roulette and dice. She planned on getting slot machines, too, but they managed to shut her down before she got to that. Bobbi's was the first Indian casino. It worked sort of the way her tribe had fishing rights, contrary to Washington State law: because Indian nations are sovereign entities not under state law. A nation within a nation, as it were. Gambling was against the law in Washington State, but it didn't or wasn't supposed to matter. Washington State had no jurisdiction on Indian land. And the feds do only insofar as federal crimes are concerned.

Her casino was spectacularly successful but the state somehow managed to close her down after a little more than a year. It was widely rumored Bobbi had Mafia backing.

Because her mousy little secretary, Alice Frye, disappeared at the same time, it was also widely believed, according to the supermarket tabloids, that Bobbi and Alice were "lesbian lovers" who had skipped town together.

Then Alice returned to Seattle several weeks later claiming she had been visiting relatives on the Lummi Reservation and they had gone out to one of the uninhabited San Juan Islands on a sort of spiritual retreat and she wasn't aware anyone regarded her as missing. Her relatives vouched for her. She didn't even know, she said, that Bobbi had jumped bail. But, Alice told the press, she was convinced of Bobbi's innocence. And that Washington State, the FBI, the BIA, and a lot of other representatives of the American government had it in for Bobbi and were persecuting her because they just couldn't stand it that a poor Indian, and a *woman* Indian at that, made it big in the white man's world. Alice Frye added that even well-meaning white liberals only liked Indians as long as they remained downtrodden, as long as they had a "plight" and were "vanishing Americans." But if they become wealthy and successful? Forget about it!

Alice Frye had no notion of the whereabouts of her former longtime employer and beloved friend.

I am going to write down everything I can recall about Bobbi. Tomorrow morning I'll write queries to several publishing houses. One of them has to bite. One just has to! Bobbi T. and her troubles with the FBI is a hot topic. Headline news.

Maybe, just maybe, my days of poverty are coming to an end!

I am broke. Or just about. I am down to $2,000 and have no prospects. Except Barb, who will hire me, she said, to do typing for her at minimum wage. "Don't be too proud, Lena," she advised. But I have a good chance of making serious money here. Nothing wrong with making money. A writer, unlike a priest, takes no vow of poverty.

It was January and extremely cold in Windsor, Ontario. I had been sleeping in the Micmac couple's garage for several days and eating at least one meal a day at their table.

They were poor and had little to share. And they were drunkards. I did things for them to make it worth their while to let me stick around: washed their laundry and chopped the wood for their wood-burning stove. I swept and mopped their floors.

I met them at a dive of an Indian bar in Detroit and told them some sob story or another; I think I said I was a battered woman running from my brute of a husband who had an uncanny ability to track me down. That explained why I wanted to lie low. Hah! As if I would ever be a pitiful battered woman. Any man who would dare lay a hand on me would be a dead man.

I wondered if the Micmacs turned me in hoping to collect the $20,000 reward the FBI offered for information leading to my arrest and conviction. "We had no idea she was Roberta Trumaine," they said in one paper. The RCMPs descended upon their home like a swarm of locust that cold, dark morning. "We thought she was just some poor Indian down on her luck and we were helping how we could. That's how we Indians are." The Micmacs went on Hard Copy *and sold their story to* The National Inquirer.

I lay there in my bed fully dressed in a T-shirt, jeans, wool socks, and a black-and-red checked flannel shirt waiting for daylight, thinking about nothing except how cold I was and how badly I needed a bath. The Micmacs didn't have a door on their bathroom. And the tub looked as though it hadn't been scrubbed out for some time. I'd asked the Micmacs if they would let me put their door back on its hinges and if they didn't have an extra blanket I could use. The quilt they'd given me was very dirty with grease spots on it as though it had been used to lie on under a car while doing mechanical repairs. It was too old to wash, they'd said. It would just disintegrate in the washing machine. It smelled of dog and some other rancid odor. Maybe butter, a lot of it, had once melted on it and spoiled. I'd feel more comfortable if I had a clean blanket between me and this quilt.

I lived the moment of my arrest hundreds, maybe thousands, of times in my imagination. When it arrived it was anticlimactic. Sort of the way a movie is hyped and you get so you want to see it really bad and are expecting what all the advertisements have led you to expect: a colossal film more entertaining, more timely, more artistic than any you've ever seen before. And your imagination is set loose and you eagerly await its release. Then, when you do see it, even though it might sweep the Academy Awards and get loads of critical praise, it still can't live up to your expectations. Nothing could.

That's how it was, anticlimactic. There was a surreal quality to it when the RCMP kicked in the garage door as I lay there in the dark in my bed. A round, smooth-faced Anglo-looking RCMP stood in the doorway pointing a gun straight at me. "Roberta Regina, you are under arrest." The cop stepped aside, still pointing the gun at me, as two more officers walked through the doorway, stepping on the flimsy, broken-down door and moving towards me. Both of their guns were drawn too. "Put your hands up in the air where we can see them. Don't make a move until we tell you." I noticed that cop, the first one who kicked the door down, wore lipstick and eyebrow pencil. She was a woman. I didn't know women could be RCMPs. Doesn't seem right. But then desperadoes are sometimes women. I didn't know they wore blue uniforms, either. Mounties are supposed to be men in red uniforms and black boots like Sergeant Preston of the Yukon. They probably didn't even ride horses anymore. I put my hands up. The woman RCMP had called me "Roberta Regina," my first and middle name, forgetting my surname. She must be very nervous. I hoped she didn't accidentally pull the trigger. "We have you surrounded."

They cuffed my wrists together behind my back and led me outside and put me in the back of a paddy wagon. The Micmacs stood on their porch in their pajamas looking, as usual, very hungover. The wife hadn't put her dentures in yet. Some of their neighbors had come outside in the subzero weather to stand in the dim early morning light on the hard frozen snow to watch the show. Others just stared from their windows.

Being captured was a relief. A big relief. In my worst-imagined scenario the feds got me and did me the way they did AIM leader Anna Mae Aquash. Some believe the FBI killed Anna Mae. Including me. Circumstantial evidence pointed to the feds but they were never charged, of course. They cut off her hands hoping to keep her true identity secret. They buried her quickly in an anonymous pauper's grave and wrote in their reports that they had found the body of an unidentified female transient who had died of "exposure."

But, as luck would have it, the Mounties got me instead. Whew!

And now the running was over at long last. I didn't resist. I went quietly. Later I read some newspaper reports that said according to RCMP officers I "seemed resigned" to my fate. Hah! I was calm not resigned. They didn't know I had an ace up my sleeve. If those Micmacs were expecting Canadian authorities to just fork me over to the FBI, to fork over the reward money to them, well, they had another think coming! I won't be leaving Canada anytime soon.

Bobbi T. is a cause célèbre! She petitioned the Canadian government for political asylum. That was all it took.

AIM radical Leonard Peltier was caught in Canada too. The FBI told blatant lies. Canada extradited Peltier. When Canada found out, it publicly confronted the Feds, who readily admitted their lies. Sure they lied! They would have used any means possible to get Peltier back. Canada was understandably very miffed.

Now here was another American Indian whom the FBI had had a file on for twenty odd years, ever since the sixties when she demonstrated along with the rest of the Indian fishermen in

Washington state's fish-ins. Bobbi T. got a lot of press then because she was the only woman among the Indians who made their living fishing their "accustomed" waters, as was the right according to the treaties. But Washington State was forever arresting and fining them, refusing to recognize the federal treaties. Two of my brothers-in-law were active in that movement. I remembered Bobbi from the olden days, when I was in my early teens.

Bobbi was quite striking then. She had a long, loose mane of raven-black hair and strong Indian features and was often photographed and interviewed on television. She was only a little heavy back then but, as time passed and she grew wealthier and wealthier, she became very heavy indeed, as though her weight had to be in proportion to her wealth. Bobbi was no longer an activist after she became a businesswoman, but she made an appearance at Wounded Knee and on Alcatraz Island during its occupation by Indians of All Tribes.

Photographs of Bobbi with Marlon Brando, Paul Newman, Jane Fonda, Dick Gregory, and Buffy St. Marie made the newspapers and sometimes the international wire services. And now the lying FBI wanted her extradited. It was not at all implausible to the Canadians that, like Peltier, Bobbi was the target of political persecution. Canada was reviewing her case and that could conceivably take seven or eight years. In the meantime Bobbi came to British Columbia to live. She isn't going to leave Canada anytime soon.

The Indian community in western Canada rallied around Bobbi. Indian politicians welcomed her and issued statements criticizing the American government and its bad treatment of its Indians. A son of a traditional chief, a popular entertainer, held a big ceremony down at the Vancouver Indian Center in which he adopted Bobbi as his blood sister and pledged his support.

It was a fine celebration, drums and traditional singing and dancing and a salmon feast. Bobbi looked good, long and lean and suntanned. For all her hardships she looked a good ten years younger than her sixty years. Her wild black mane was gone. Now her hair was salt-and-pepper gray and cut very short.

I couldn't get near her the day of her adoption but I spoke to her secretary, Alice, who was once again by her side. I told Alice who I was and she said she'd read both my novels and admired them very much. I told her I wanted to write a book about Bobbi. Alice gave me a phone number that I had to pledge I'd never let another soul know. She said to call early the following week.

By then I'd read all the newspaper and magazine articles about Bobbi I could get my hands on and I'd painstakingly remembered and pondered all I knew about her and now I looked forward with great excitement to meeting and talking with her. Even though I might not ever write the nonfiction book I had in mind.

I heard from editors at three of the publishing houses I'd contacted and the news wasn't good.

Peter Matthiessen wrote a book, *In the Spirit of Crazy Horse*, about AIM and AIMs troubles with the FBI. I bought that book when it first came out back in '82. Matthiessen wrote about Anna Mae Aquash's strange death, how her hands were cut off and her body was buried in a pauper's grave as "an unidentified female transient" at first.

He wrote about the arson fire that killed John Trudell's mother-in-law, wife, and three kids and how it was never proven who did it. But the obvious suspect, it seems to me, is the FBI. He interviewed the hardcore Indian criminal Robert Hugh Wilson who upon his oath deposed and said that when he and Peltier were both prisoners at Marion, Illinois, the chief correctional officer brought a "well-dressed stranger in a light brown suit and a diagonal striped tie" to his room at the prison hospital who told Wilson that if he would cooperate in "neutralizing" Peltier he would see to it Wilson received the medical attention he needed and that he would be paroled from the federal prison system to his Oklahoma detainer. When Wilson asked "the stranger" in the brown suit who he was and what he meant by "neutralizing" Peltier, the stranger identified himself only as "a person who has the power to do what I promise" and that Wilson would have to "weigh for himself" what was meant by "neutralizing." Wilson, after a time, agreed, he said, to participate in an assassination plot.

In the spring of '83, a few months after Peter Matthiessen's book came out, former South Dakota Governor William Janklow sued Matthiessen and Viking Press for libel to the tune of $24 million. Then, in '84, both author and publisher were sued by Special Agent David Price of the FBI for $25 million. What I heard is that because Price assured Matthiessen in his interview that he never made a move without the approval of his superiors, and since an FBI agent's salary isn't enough to pay for the very expensive attorneys he retained, Matthiessen assumed the FBI itself sponsored the suit.

The case won't be decided, most likely, for several more years. It isn't expected Matthiessen and Viking will win. In the meantime, publishers are intimidated. They all steer clear of any material that might bring about a similar suit.

It doesn't matter to me now, though, because something exciting has happened: I am writing, really writing, again. Hallelujah! Obsessed again. Possessed. The process is everything. It is what matters. Nothing is better than this. Nothing makes me feel so alive.

My interest in Bobbi, though, hasn't diminished since I found out nobody would give me an advance and nobody would even be likely to publish a book about her if I wrote one. I want to meet and talk with her still. I want to find out more.

Alice told me an Indian woman, a writer, wants to talk with me about writing a book on my life. She said she was Wes' cousin's wife's sister and used to play with Wes Junior and Claudia when they were all children, back in the days when me, my mom, Wes, and the kids all lived in a little two-room house before Wes ran off with his first woman, before I became the fisher in our family. I don't remember this woman at all. Lena. I remember her family, though. They came from somewhere else, Montana or Idaho. Somewhere like that.

Lots of Indians from other places settle in or near Seattle and become part of the Indian community. Their children marry Coast Indians. I suppose because the Northwest Coast is a good place to live.

If I play my cards right, Lena will write a book that will set things right. Tell my version of the story. The word according to Bobbi.

Bobbi and Alice welcomed me to the house one of Bobbi's supporters let them have as a home and headquarters. To tell the truth, it wasn't hard to see why there were rumors concerning their relationship. They seemed like a loving couple, happy to be together again. Alice beamed at Bobbi in a frankly adoring way. Whatever their relationship, whether they were cousins (Bobbi told me Alice was her cousin and secretary), employee and employer, devoted friends, or lovers, it was their own personal business. I had no intention of asking anything about it.

We made small talk at first. Bobbi remembered my parents, she said, and my sisters. She remembered my brother, whom I didn't remember that well. He joined the army when he was seventeen and never came home again. He was killed in Vietnam. I told Bobbi I was sorry about her daughter Claudia's death. A dark shadow passed over Bobbi's face a moment as she was reminded of Claudia. Alice reached over and put her hand over Bobbi's and squeezed it. Claudia, who was my age, died when she was in her twenties. Everyone said it was a drug overdose. I never heard anything different.

Alice served iced tea and then excused herself.

I told Bobbi what the editors told me, how, since *In the Spirit of Crazy Horse,* they were all afraid to publish anything that would in any way say anything bad about the FBI or any arm of the American government. But that I was fascinated by her story and wanted to write it even though it might not go anyplace. She nodded her head. She understood. She told me she'd been approached by other writers but she wanted an Indian writer to tell her story. I told her I'd be back, if it was all right with her, with some interview questions and we could get started.

"There's one thing I want to get straight right off the bat," Bobbi said, startling me. "I am not now nor have I ever been a lesbian. That bullshit about Alice and me being lovers made me the angriest of all the bullshit I read about myself." Bobbi's face was flushed in anger. "It made me angrier, even, than all that stuff about how I was 'hugely obese' and all those ugly pictures they printed that showed me looking like a pig. I was never that fat, you know, not like the press would have it. Sure I weighed more than three-hundred pounds, but I'm a good-sized woman, you know. Nearly six feet tall and big-boned. For the record, I am *not* a lesbian. I don't know how they could even write that stuff. On the one hand, they have me hiring a hit man to polish off Leona Garr for fooling around with my old man. On the other, they have me carrying on a torrid affair with Alice! What a bunch of assholes!"

I wasn't aware of Lena's existence, but she looked a lot like her pretty sisters and that brother, Carl. He was awfully good looking and I had a crush on him way back when. Before I married Wes. Before Lena was born. That goes to show, doesn't it, that I was always heterosexual?

Sometimes, when I was on the lam, I'd think of Alice and how much I missed her. And, yes, how I loved her. How she was the truest friend I ever had and I'd give anything to have her near me. To see her face and hear her voice. And I'd have my doubts. Was I, deep down, really a lesbian? One of those latent lesbians?

I'll never forget the first time I saw little Alice. We were young, Alice and me, in those days. One rainy week night, quite late, Alice came in the

Sasquatch. I was tending bar. The only people there were a couple of drunks drinking beer and playing pool. Alice was drenched. That made her look even littler and skinnier.

Alice ordered a drink. Then another. Then another. She was getting pretty drunk. Finally she ran out of money. She ordered it and I served it to her, but she couldn't come up with the two dollars. She put a dollar bill on the bar then began searching her bag for change. Found a dime. Then a couple of pennies. "Miss," I said, "maybe you've had enough. Maybe you should go on home now. I hope you aren't driving." She burst into tears.

"I don't have a car," she said. "I don't even have a home." I took Alice home with me that night and let her sleep on the sofa. The next day she told me she'd been drinking an awful lot for the past eighteen months and just couldn't seem to stop. She'd lost her job as a clerk at Stadium High School because of her drinking. I had experience with drunks because of Wes. I called AA and found out where the next meeting was and drove Alice to her first AA meeting. She really took to AA and never had another drink since that night she came into my bar looking like a little drowned rat.

Alice stayed with me and tended bar. She began keeping books. By the time my casino opened she was my personal secretary. It seems as though Alice has always been with me. I rely on her a great deal.

The last time I saw Alice before she showed up in Ontario was after I convinced her to go home. I didn't want to see her off. I thought we were easy pickings *for those who hunted us: A tall, very large Indian woman and a short, slight Indian woman who was part Chinese and wore thick glasses. We said good-bye at the motel.*

We had never had any physical contact until our fond good-bye. "I'll pray for you every day, Bobbi," she said, her eyes all welled up. (Alice is a devout Catholic and served as a lay missionary in Alaska.) Then she put her arms around me and hugged me. "I love you," she said. "I'll always love you." And for some reason I started bawling too. Then we laughed and blew our noses and wiped the tears away and she picked up her suitcase and opened the door and walked out of my life. I wept for hours. Life as I knew it was over.

Then, when they brought me in five years later, there was Alice! She came to Ontario and waited around a whole week before they allowed her to see me. We had to talk on phones facing each other through a bullet-proof window. She'd be waiting, she told me. She had ten thousand dollars saved up. She was there to take care of me.

Later on, after my release, after we got settled into this house, when we were just sitting around drinking wine one evening, Alice told me that she was neither homosexual nor heterosexual. She was asexual. She could not recall ever having any sexual feelings.

Then she told me a horror story about being repeatedly raped and sodomized by her grandfather when she was five years old. He said he'd kill her if she told. Then her grandfather died and she prayed to God thanking Him. She went to school, which she loved because it took her away from home. Even the taunts of the other kids didn't phase her much. (Alice had very poor eyesight. She wore glasses that magnified her little, almond-shaped eyes and she had skinny, twig-like legs. One of the names the kids at school called her was "Bird Legs.") She loved school because she loved learning and the more she learned the stronger and more powerful she felt.

When she was nine her stepfather began molesting her and continued to do so until her mother kicked him out, without ever knowing what was going on. Then one of her mother's drunkard boyfriends got into bed with her one night after her mother passed out.

He made her perform oral sex on him. Made her swallow his semen. If she told her mother, he said, her mother would never believe her. Alice didn't sleep after that when her mother and her boyfriend drank and didn't ever sleep well. The boyfriend eventually stole into her room again one night.

This time Alice was prepared. She had taken a big butcher knife from the kitchen and used a whet stone to sharpen the edge, honing it for hours until it was very sharp indeed. Then she took it to bed every night and lay there in the dark listening to the drunken couple's antics. Finally the night came when he opened little Alice's bedroom door and came in to her and lay down on her bed. But she'd slid out of bed as soon as she heard him at the door. Now she stood over him. She could see him well in the faint light that spilled in from the hallway through the open door. She took the handle of the *knife and raised it above her head and brought it down full force into his throat. Then out. And into his abdomen. Then she tried to stab him in the heart but wasn't strong enough to drive the blade through his ribs. She could hear the gurgling sound the blood made in his throat. She felt oddly calm.*

The authorities believed her when she told them what happened. The boyfriend had several convictions for child rape.

The authorities took Alice away from her mother, who refused to believe her boyfriend had molested her daughter. Alice was some kind of bad seed, she said. A killer child. Alice, she said, killed the only man she ever loved and then made up that story. Alice's mother didn't want to ever see Alice again.

From that time on, until she turned eighteen, Alice lived in foster homes. And she had never desired, she told me, not ever, to touch or be touched in an erotic way. That didn't make her a lesbian. She never had sex with a woman. She never had sex.

Alice and I are not lesbian lovers. But we are dear friends. Loving friends. Alice is really all I have. I want her to stay with me now. From now on. I hope we'll never be separated again.

The day I was to begin interviewing Bobbi, my friend Barb called me on the phone.

"Hi Lena. Hey, did you hear the news about Roberta Trumaine?" I hadn't. "She had a massive heart attack this morning. She's in critical condition. It sounds awfully serious."

I wasn't able to find out which hospital had Bobbi. I learned later it was the one down in White Rock. Peace Arch Hospital. She and Alice had gone down there because it is a pleasant, picturesque little town. They went to little antique shops, walked on the beach, and talked about settling there when all the fuss died down and they had jobs and money. Bobbi told Alice she had a good feeling about the book I was going to write. It would be a bestseller and would be made into a major motion picture. If they couldn't find an Indian actress to portray her, she hoped Sigourney Weaver got the part. She and Alice would have money. Everything was going to be fine in the end.

They ate at a Greek taverna where a male belly dancer performed suggestively, right up to tables where women sat. Some of them tucked bills in his harem pants as he rotated his pelvis around in their faces. Alice and Bobbi left. That wasn't their cup of tea.

They walked out on the pier. It was such a lovely summer night. They stood at the end of the pier and looked out over the water. Then, suddenly, Bobbi collapsed. Alice ran back down the pier and called an ambulance from the taverna. She was sure Bobbi was a goner. She prayed as she'd never prayed before. Bobbi pulled through and in time was home again, recuperating.

I called in October and arranged a visit. Alice said I'd have to limit my time to twenty minutes and I was not to bring up anything that might upset Bobbi. Like Leona Garr and the alleged murder attempt. Like her daughter Claudia who died or her son Wes Jr. who was his father's son and condemned his mother for having screwed up his head early on. Don't ask her about the Mafia. Don't ask her how she managed to survive those years on the run. But please do come by. Bobbi often speaks of Lena and says she wishes Lena would visit.

I had good news to tell Bobbi and Alice. Random House bought the hardcover rights to my novel and nominated it for a raft of prizes. It would be coming out soon. The launching would be at the Native Education Center where my friend Barb teaches the Git San language. Random House is sending me on an eighteen-city publicity tour.

It is always a let down when one finishes a book. It's gone then. That world you've created, all the characters you've grown used to living with. I imagine postpartum depression is sort of like that. There will be a big hole in my life now until I begin another novel. *If* I ever write another novel. Maybe all my books were flukes.

I did hire a shooter, not to kill Leona Garr but to scare her. The woman wouldn't let go of Wes. Called him several times a day. Hung up if I answered. Wrote me a letter telling me if I really loved Wes I'd set him free. She even came to my home and confronted me. I told her to go away or I might well kill her. Of course I wouldn't have.

One of my kitchen help told me he knew some-one who could take care of the Leona problem. Permanently. I hired him to scare her. That's all. Only a very lame hit man would shoot four times at a woman all alone on a dark country road and miss. All that other stuff I don't recall much. I remember being rich. I remember going to Africa to see Muhammad Ali fight. Lot of rich stuff. I loved being rich. It could have all been a fantasy, though. It all seems like another life now. Lena asked how it felt to lose my wealth and become a person so poor I didn't have enough to eat and sometimes no place to crash. Sort of like a return to childhood. To the simplicity of childhood. All I want, really, is peace.

Alice and I are happy together. Vancouver is a good place to live. It will be a good place to die.

Bobbi never became strong again after the first heart attack. When I visited her in October, she didn't look anything like the Bobbi I knew. She looked old and tired, all ashen-faced. She'd regained about thirty pounds or so. She looked like she'd aged ten years.

The Micmac couple who let her sleep in their garage in Ontario brought charges against her. They said their ten-year-old daughter had told them Bobbi molested her. The Indian commu-nity renounced Bobbi then, as quickly as it had welcomed her before. She and Alice had to move out of the comfortable house and into a wretched little hotel downtown. Bobbi had to go to Ontario for her arraignment.

The Micmacs' daughter wasn't even there when Bobbi stayed with them. She and Alice believed the FBI had gotten to them. Maybe they gave them money. Maybe it was something else they'd needed which the feds had the power to give them.

Bobbi, after a twenty-year cessation, took up smoking again. She took to staying up late drinking coffee and smoking cigarettes and watching late night TV. Alice found her dead one morning sitting in her Goodwill Industries chair before the TV. Alice refused to let Bobbi's relatives take her back to Seattle for burial. Alice had her cremated. Alice and Barb and I scattered her ashes in Stanley Park near the place the Hudson's Bay ship, the *Beaver*, sank. Alice said a Catholic prayer.

Several years have passed since Bobbi T. died. Alice stayed on in Vancouver. I run into her every once in awhile. The last time was at the theater where Barb and Ramon (a man Barb was seeing for awhile) and I went to see a South African play with an all-woman cast, *When You Strike the Woman You Strike the Stone*. Alice, who now teaches computer classes and business English part time at the Native Ed Centre, brought several young women students to see the play.

I am forty-three now and, since settling down with Tom, the mail carrier, I am considering having a baby. But what if I can't raise a child? What if I end up doing to my child what was done to me by my family? Or what if the child doesn't love me, like Wes Jr. didn't love Bobbi T.? What would I do then?

Tommy, who is divorced and has to cough up half his salary in child support payments, would just as soon not have another child. That's what he tells me when he hints about marriage.

What if Tommy runs out on me the way all my other men have?

I am halfway through another novel. A non-literary thriller. The protagonist is a social worker in Seattle. Mary Kay has become disillusioned with welfare cheats and slumlords and sexual abusers of children and battered women who truly do bring it upon themselves.

Mary Kay desperately wants to live a freer, more sheltered life. She starts to have blackouts during which she apparently sleepwalks. Now someone is murdering welfare recipients, every one of them on *her* caseload. The murderer leaves messages written in blood on walls: "Thank me, society! I have rid you of yet another parasite!"

She arrives at the low-rent apartment of Barnaby Hugo, one of her most disgusting clients, to find the door wide open. She steps inside, walks down the short hall, then sees Hugo's dead and decapitated body lying on the floor. She sees his head on the floor against the wall, his facial features arranged in an idiotic grin. Above his head is a dialogue balloon such as in comic books. Written in blood inside the balloon: "Hi, everyone. Thank Mary Kay for putting me out of my misery. I won't be raping any more little girls. See you in hell!" Mary Kay hears sirens. She looks out the eighth-story window and sees her boss and a uniformed policeman get out of cars and walk up the front steps of the apartment building. Mary Kay runs to the bathroom and squeezes through a small window. Thank God she's as slim as Bridget Fonda.

Mary Kay, a high school athlete, is still very agile. She jumps to the next building, runs across the roof, and climbs down the fire escape to the alley below. By now cops are all over. She finds a passed-out bum in the alley whose coat and hat she borrows and then steals right past the stupid cops. Then she runs away and hides out in a wooded area until dark. She sneaks to the back door of her best friend Christine's apartment. But, just as she is about to knock, she looks through the window and sees Christine and her boss, Dan Reed, having passionate sex on Christine's kitchen table. Mary Kay now suspects Reed. And maybe Christine is in cahoots with him. The only other person she can trust is the man she recently dumped, a Joe Mantegna look-alike named Nick. Nick is a chronic depressive who has attempted suicide more than once or twice. Mary Kay loved him but decided she had enough of her own troubles without linking up with someone who was always down and wanting to die. Now he is the only one who can help her.

The social worker must find the real murderer in order to clear herself. It could be the rookie she has been training who is overly idealistic and appalled at every disgusting thing she sees on the job.

It could be her rival, Mary Jo Fortensky, who had been at the agency five years longer than Mary Kay but was recently passed over for promotion.

It could be old Mrs. Alphonse, one of the recipients who once was a social worker but was beaten so badly by one of the low-lifes on her caseload that she sustained brain damage and is prone to seizures.

The obvious suspect, so obvious that Mary Kay doesn't really suspect him, is a grumpy young man, Walter, who was hired on a short while ago after completing his MSW.

Walter was forever calling the ne'er-do-wells slime balls, scrotum bags, prick heads, schmucks, bags of shit, etc. He hated any and all who had to turn to social service agencies for help for any reason. Mary Kay had gone out with him for after-work drinks. Walter had gotten drunk and told her that he had been raised on welfare himself by a teenaged unwed mother who made a little extra money turning tricks. He had hated his mother and women like her all of his life. When he was a little boy he'd wanted to be Batman when he grew up. Then, when he found out this was an unrealistic career goal, he'd wanted to be a supercop, only he had fallen arches and lost his hearing in one ear after he fell through the icy surface of a lake he was skating on one winter day. So he decided he could best combat evil by becoming a social worker. And there he was.

Though Mary Kay could hardly stand the thought, she realizes, God forbid, it really *could* be her. She could be the murderer, commit murder during blackouts then blocking it out of her conscious awareness.

This is my first murder mystery thriller. The other four were all literary works, which is where my heart is. But I need money. And why not admit it? I am in the thrall of my own story. I must solve the puzzle. But what will I do when it's done?

I could write the Bobbi T. story now that the FBI has lost its suit against Peter Mathiessen and his publisher and *In the Spirit of Crazy Horse* has been released again. But I have never written nonfiction. And I never got a chance to discuss important issues with Bobbi. I don't know whether or not Bobbi tried to have Leona Garr whacked. Of course Bobbi claimed to be innocent of *all* charges.

Everyone knew Leona was forever having affairs with married men. Any one of them or their wives could have hired a shooter or taken pot shots at her. Or Leona's oft-cuckolded husband could have finally gotten fed up and shot at her himself. What would Bobbi have said? Probably that she, not a hired shooter, shot at Leona but it was in self-defense. Leona was coming at her with an icepick, thinking that Wes would belong to her once Bobbi, the obstacle to their love, was out of the picture.

I didn't get a chance to ask Bobbi about the Mafia or the racketeering.

Maybe I'll write a novel based on Bobbi T. Make Bobbi a man. Maybe Leona would turn up shot to death and "Bob," her former lover who was trying to get rid of her, who had even said in front of witnesses, "Stay away from me and my family or so help me God, I will kill you!" would stand accused of her murder. Then he'd have to take it on the lam before his arrest. Or break out of jail. Or jump bail.

Then he'd have to find the real murderer in order to clear himself. And, though "Bob" was something of a womanizer and had had affairs with lots of glamorous models and starlets and whatnot, the one woman he knows he can rely on and (he is well aware) has had a long-standing crush on him is his skinny, homely little secretary, Hilda. Together Bob and Hilda set about finding Leona's killer.

I can set everything right. Bobbi's daughter Claudia could go to rehab and quit using and be alive and happy today. I could rename Bobbi's husband Wes "Wynona." Maybe "Wynona" could be a composite of Wes and Jeremy, my own unfaithful ex-husband. Wynona and one of her promiscuous playmates could suffer an unfortunate accident after smoking in bed. Then, in their exile, "Bob" and "Hilda" would have the insurance money to live on and "Bob" would realize it was really she, Hilda, his faithful secretary, whom he has loved all along. In my novel

Bob and Hilda, unlike Bobbi and Alice, can consummate their love.

For now, back to Mary Kay and Nick. Mary Kay disguises herself as a loony lady and goes into a loony bin. She is Nick's crazy "Cousin" Isobel. Nick gets her out of the psych ward but cannot support her, of course, since he is only able to hold jobs between his episodes of severe depression. And "Isobel" is unable to work due to looniness so she and Nick go the agency to apply for aid. Mary Kay, as Isobel, is put on the caseload of the zealous young social worker, the would-be Batman, Walter.

I'm sure this one will make me some money. There's nothing wrong with wanting money. I have taken no vow of poverty.

---o---

Alice Fay

The night before Alice Fay's mother, Norma, died, Alice Fay had *the* dream. Old-time Indians believed in prophetic dreams, she thought, but wasn't sure. She was an Indian but she didn't know much about them. Anyway, if one dreamed of someone's death it was sure to come true.

In her dream she got up in the middle of the night. Everything was exactly as in real life; no weird dream landscape or anything. She slipped soundlessly out of her little room and across the carpeted living room and into Norma's room at the other end.

Norma lay sleeping, the white walls of her room lit by the moonlight and street lamps, her toothless mouth gaping open, snoring lightly. Alice Fay stood looking at her mother's sleeping face for a moment, then picked up one of the pillows from Norma's bed, and, holding it almost tenderly in both hands, lowered it.

Years later, when Alice Fay would see the film, *One Flew over the Cuckoo's Nest,* she would recall the dream, how she, like Will Sampson in the movie, pushed the pillow down firmly and held it. How long? Three minutes or four? Norma struggled at first, as Jack Nicholson would, then lay still.

Alice Fay removed the pillow, tossed it onto the wheelchair. She gazed calmly upon Norma's dead face. She reached down and closed the eyes that would never see anything again. She felt no remorse. Odd, how richly detailed this dream was.

Afterwards she just went back to her own room and into bed and snuggled into a deep sleep as if nothing had happened.

When she woke hours later in the stark light of day, she remembered with horror what she had done in the night. My God, Holy Mary Mother of God, pray for us sinners. Maybe it *was* just a dream. No, not this time. That was why she made no attempt to interrupt herself; she thought it was the dream again and so just let it run. Or, maybe it wasn't a dream and still Norma could have survived the attempt on her life. That must happen sometimes, a person only appearing to be smothered to death but later reviving.

Alice Fay slipped her feet into her scuffs and reached for her royal-blue velour robe. It was on the hook on the closed door where she hung it last night after she killed Norma. That was where she always hung her robe though. That didn't mean anything. She slipped it over her head and hurried to her mother's room. She could hear the sound of her own heartbeat in her ears.

"So there you are," Norma scowled. "Took you damned long enough!" Alice Fay looked at the clock on the wall over Norma's head. 7:02.

Seven was always the time she came to attend Norma on Saturdays. Weekdays when the aide looked after her it was about the same time too. "Hand me my bedpan! Hurry up! What the hell is the matter with you, standing there with your mouth wide open! Get the damned bedpan before I pee the bed!" Killing Norma, then, had been only a dream. First relief and then dread. Alice Fay was still her mother's prisoner and this was Saturday. She wouldn't be going off to her job at the Washington State Department of Motor Vehicles *this* morning. Mariann wouldn't be coming in today. Or tomorrow either.

➤◉➤
Alice Fay

Alice Fay got the bedpan for Norma, who had never allowed her to call her mother. Norma lifted herself and let Alice Fay slip the stainless steel pan under her now scrawny, toneless butt. "Why aren't you dressed yet?" she said as the tinny sound of pee hitting metal began. "You still have to clean this pigsty, then give me my bath. Did you forget Tilly's coming to visit? Get the lead out, woman!"

Alice Fay took a shower first. Norma could just set her own full bedpan onto her wheelchair, even though she wanted it to be taken away, emptied, and rinsed immediately. Let her deal with it.

Today Alice Fay took her time. Maybe she wouldn't even vacuum. She had forgotten Norma's sister Tilly was visiting today. She came at least one Saturday a month, sometimes every other week. That meant Alice Fay would have respite after all. (Norma hated to be left alone in the apartment for even an hour.) Alice Fay sat at her dressing table and applied makeup to her round little Indian face. She outlined her eyes with dramatic black liquid liner. (She still had a child's face though she was thirty. Makeup helped.) She twisted the cap on her little bottle of liquid base (almond now in the middle of winter, later on suntan). Norma still made her face up sometimes. Her base was ivory, and once Norma had been beautiful. Alice Fay turned on the radio. Diana Ross and the Supremes sang "Stop in the Name of Love!"

Alice Fay, who was named by Granny Gloria after some old movie star, had lived with sickly great-granny most of the first five years of her life. (Norma's mother had died when Norma and Tilly were little girls and Granny Gloria had raised both of them, too.) Alice Fay almost never stayed with Norma. Once in awhile Norma left her with other relatives, whose names and faces she could no longer remember. Sometimes she even left her with strangers she met in bars. Alice Fay was always glad to be with Granny, who was little, skinny, poor, and frugal.

Sometimes Granny Gloria and Alice Fay would gather beer and soda pop bottles from the sides of the road. Once, after gathering bottles all day long, they made six dollars! Granny Gloria bought Alice Fay a Little Lulu funny book that day.

Granny had a friend, an old man, who was caretaker at the Tacoma City Dump. Mr. Fisher gave them all kinds of good things he'd salvaged: a nice mahogany coffee table, clothing, sometimes even canned food. Alice Fay remembered once he gave them a whole bagful of miniature Hershey's and Mr. Goodbar chocolate bars. She and Granny had eaten only two each evening and made their candy stash last a long while. Mr. Fisher told them once a long time ago he'd found a diamond ring, and if he found another, he'd give it to Alice Fay. She kept waiting for the longest time and daydreaming and longing for a diamond ring.

Granny's house, in a rural area outside Tacoma, was covered with black tarpaper and had a tin roof. Its ceiling was so low inside Norma and Tilly's heads almost touched it. Granny grew rose bushes in the front and there the grass was thick, green, and overgrown. She fenced in the dirt backyard, though, and kept chickens there. For company, Alice Fay supposed, since they did not lay eggs and Granny would never think of killing "the girls" and eating them. They were old ladies just like her and she'd had them since before Alice Fay was born. In summer Granny left the back door open and the girls had the run of the house. They liked to nest in easy chairs. Alice Fay didn't know how many chickens Granny had had to begin with, but when they died, she and Granny would bury them in the back yard and even say a few words over them. By the time Alice Fay was five and went away to St. Jude Catholic Indian Mission

Boarding School, only Dolores—Dee—and Josie were left.

"The first time I laid eyes on you, Honeybunch," Granny told her, "you were about six weeks old. And you were the cutest little papoose Indian baby girl I ever saw. I went on out to that reservation. Oh Lord, musta taken me ten hours to get there, and then it was dark and I didn't know where I was goin' and it was winter, too cold to sleep in the car, so I had to get a room at the motel. The next day I asked around town. Folks knew your daddy's place and gave me directions.

"I set out like that to find you and Norma because I knew how she got. Her depressions and all. She had already tried to commit suicide once with sleeping pills. I wrote her letters that weren't answered and weren't returned either. I got scared. The last letter I got from her was in November, two months before you was due. Norma described her life as hell. How did she end up married to some red Indian fellah, living in a hellhole with her belly as big as a watermelon? She couldn't see her toes let alone reach them. Her man clipped her toenails for her. She said her husband had hunting knives with sharp blades that tempted her, and sometimes she imagined getting tanked up on whiskey, then going outside to take a nap in the snow.

"Of course I had to go looking for her. I don't know how it was she took up with your daddy. She never said and I never asked. The house sure was a hellhole all right! No running water or electric lights, miles and miles out in the country, all set off by itself. When I drove up a bunch of damned dogs surrounded my car growling and barking. Your daddy appeared in the doorway holding you in one arm, a metal spatula in the other. He'd been cooking, I guess.

"I told him I was Norma's grandmother and he took me back to the bedroom to see her. My beautiful girl looked like some kind of damned ghost. I swear. She just lay there quiet. She didn't even answer when I spoke to her. I knew it wasn't physical. I knew. The depressions. That's why Norma always had to keep moving like she did and couldn't settle down. The depressions would catch up with her if she did.

"I offered to take her home with me. She never did think much of the home I'd made for her, you know. Never thought much of me, if the truth were known. 'Take that baby away,' she said, turning her face towards the wall.

"I asked your daddy what your name was and he said Norma hadn't felt up to naming you yet. When she got well they would give you a proper name. But he liked 'Sarah' and that was what he'd been calling you since you were born. Kind of Jewish sounding, ain't it, for a papoose baby? Naw, Sarah would never do, I thought, but kept it to myself. I held out my arms and he gave you to me and you know, darlin', I just fell in love with you. If the truth were known, I didn't know how I would feel about an Indian grandbaby or great-grandbaby. But it didn't matter if you wasn't white. Oh, you had such pretty, thick black hair and long black eyelashes.

"I loved you from the start. My own little papoose baby doll. My Ali Fay. I got him to let me take you by telling him Norma was too sick and weak to care for you and he was a man and had to get to work. I'd bring you home, I said, when Norma got well. Of course, just like I knew, she left him soon after.

"The next time I saw her she was her own beautiful, lively self again. Dropped by the place with her new man, a bald-headed Montana rancher. They'd both had a few. She stayed with that fella for nearly two years, a record for her.

"Once, when she lived in Montana, when Barbara Stanwyck was making *Cattle Queen of Montana* there, Norma got pulled over by the police and hauled in. See, Miss Stanwyck was very high-strung and she'd had a row with somebody on the set and ran off and they were scared she'd commit suicide. Hauled Norma in because they thought she was Miss Stanwyck and wouldn't believe her when she said she wasn't. Imagine. Only Norma was prettier than Barbara Stanwyck: taller, younger, blonder. But, everyone agreed, there was a resemblance."

When Alice Fay was little she thought her mother was the most beautiful woman in the world and Aunt Tilly the second. By the time she was six she was painfully aware of how different she was from them and felt like a pudgy black beetle bug compared to them.

Norma insisted that she call her Norma. She didn't want anyone to know, she said, that she had a child Alice Fay's age. In fact, being a mother would make her seem less desirable. Alice Fay, when she was older, thought it probably also had something to do with her brown skin and the racial difference between herself and her golden-girl mother. She was Norma's only child. Aunt Tilly was childless.

Alice Fay cleaned her mother's room quickly, then brought in the dishpan to sponge bathe her. Because of the stroke, Norma was paralyzed on the left side and couldn't give herself a proper bath, but managed on weekdays. The aide, Mariann, said she'd gladly bathe her, but Norma resisted: she didn't like strangers seeing her naked, she said. Alice Fay would do it on her day off.

Alice Fay washed her mother and combed her thin, grey hair. She dressed her in a fresh red satin bed jacket. It was a gift from Alice Fay. It reminded her of a form-fitting red satin dress Norma once had. No, it was a suit, not a dress. Low-necked form-fitting red satin suit. The downstairs doorbell rang and Alice Fay ran and pressed the buzzer.

"Hey come back here, you!" Norma called after her in her cracked old woman's voice. Alice Fay returned to Norma's room.

"You forgot the cologne. Spray some of the gardenia cologne on me and then, quick, get the sherry and some glasses. Pour Tilly and me some sherry." She sprayed cologne on her mother.

"I didn't say douse me in it, dammit. And take that mess away, hurry up now before she gets up here!" Alice Fay picked up Norma's bath water and washcloth and towels and dirty linens and gown and ran out of the room with them.

After the stroke, Norma's doctor told Alice Fay her mother had only from six months to a year to live—at the most, two years. There was no one to take her in and Norma had a dread of nursing homes, having worked in one once when she was young. She knew firsthand how badly nurses and attendants treated the old people. What could Alice Fay do? Norma's last marriage had ended not in divorce (the only one that didn't), but in death. As a widow of a former army colonel, she had a good pension. There would be money to hire help.

Norma *was* Alice Fay's mother. And maybe, Alice Fay hoped, Norma might come around in her helpless old age. She might say to her just before she died, "Alice Fay, I'm sorry for leaving you as I did. I was a weak person. I wasn't able to realize how precious you really were. Forgive me." And Alice Fay, tears streaming down her face, would forgive her and she would embrace her poor old mother, who would die in her arms. And then, of course, Alice Fay would have Norma's insurance money, tangible proof of her love.

Six months passed. Then a year. Then two. Ten years went by. Alice Fay turned thirty and, were it not for one encounter with a man she met at Arthur Murray's Dance Studio (she couldn't remember now what he looked like she was so used to substituting his face with Charles Bronson's when she recalled that night) before Norma came to live with her, she would be a virgin.

Her first job had been at the post office. Her second had been at the DMV, and there she was still.

When Alice Fay was not quite six years old Norma put her in St. Jude's Mission School. Any Indian kid could go there and it was free (that is, paid for by the government). It was as good a place as any to park a child.

Granny's cancer had already begun to eat away at her by then, but she visited Alice Fay whenever she could, once a month or so. Aunt Tilly and one of her husbands or boyfriends visited once in awhile too. Both Granny and Tilly brought boxes of goodies—cookies, candies, comic books (you could tell the comics Granny brought because they were old. She probably got them from Mr. Fisher, who worked at the dump. They even had a dump-like odor to them). Tilly brought good things sometimes: yo-yos, jacks, crayons, and coloring books. The nuns always confiscated the boxes as soon as the visitors left and Alice Fay never saw them or their contents again. She wondered what the nuns did with her things. She imagined them, after all the children had been put to bed, eating the confiscated treats, reading the comic books and laughing, jumping rope, playing jacks, chewing bubblegum.

She understood that Granny was sick and could no longer take care of her. "Tell Norma I'll be really, really good if she lets me live with her," she'd tell Aunt Tilly and Granny. "I'll wash dishes. I'll bring her coffee and toast every morning. I'll wash her clothes. I'll get a job. Anything. Tell her this place is a hellhole. A real hellhole, and I've been thinking of committing suicide."

Granny would shake her head at the deep bruises on Alice Fay's upper arms. "Imagine. And them so all-fired religious and all. Some brides of Jesus." Once a nun grabbed Alice Fay's arm after she'd just had a smallpox vaccination. Her whole upper arm was swollen and red, hot to the touch; a big pocket of pus formed around the vaccination. "I would take you home with me in a minute, darlin', if I wasn't so darned sick myself," Granny said.

Then Granny did not come for a long while. A spring and summer passed. Alice Fay became accustomed to the odd, mean sort of life she lived, and she herself went through a life-threatening illness.

The nuns would lock the children in a playroom for several hours after supper. Alice Fay had to pee bad. No one was there to unlock the door. She forced one of the windows open and climbed out, dropped to the ground. She ran first to the old outdoor toilets on the other side of the baseball field, where she had never been before, but these were so filthy and foul-smelling she gagged before she even stepped a foot inside.

Then she ran to the dormitory, where she and thirty other little girls slept, and where she knew at least one nun would be at this time of day. When she put her ear flat against the door she could hear someone moving about inside the dorm. Alice Fay knew she would get into trouble for escaping the playroom, but there was no helping it. She pounded desperately at the door and cried to be let in. She was ignored. She wept and pounded on the door until she bruised the side of her fist, afraid of what was going to happen. Then she felt the warm urine run down her legs. She had to sit and wait in the cold for over an hour, and that was how she got pneumonia. She was just six years old.

The winter passed and then spring and summer. One day in the fall Tilly came to tell her Granny Gloria had died, but not of cancer, as they'd all expected. Granny had been walking home one evening past dark carrying a bag of groceries. She was hit by a truck. Alice Fay remembered a cat that was run over right in front of the house; she remembered the blood and gore. Tilly said, "Don't you see, Ali, it's better this way. No long suffering. I think God was answering her prayers. Granny died instantly, probably not even aware of having been hit." And, best of all, Tilly and Norma sued the driver of the truck for wrongful death and they were each awarded $6,000, though they had been asking for and hoping for much more. Aunt Tilly bought a new car with her money, a green Buick, and took Alice

Fay for a little spin that very day. Even at age seven, Alice Fay could see this was luxury. And Norma? What did she do or what was she going to do with her $6,000? She wasn't sure. She was think of going to Las Vegas and enrolling in a dealer's school so she could get casino work.

Aunt Tilly visited Alice Fay only once more, about a year later. Norma surprised her that summer by not only visiting (her one and only visit), but bringing her "home" for a week. Norma brought her to Granny's chicken house. She had to go through Granny's things and sell the little house and the few acres of land it was on. Looking back on this time, during which Norma hardly spoke to her, Alice Fay guessed her mother was afraid, for some reason, to stay in the little chicken house alone.

Alice Fay missed Granny Gloria and liked sometimes to pretend that Granny wasn't really dead, that she was just injured and would show up, the cancer cured, better than ever, and bring her home to the chicken house to live. She knew that was just a daydream; she accepted that Granny was dead and gone and she'd never see her again, and she wasn't sorry her aunt quit visiting her and her mother never would come again. At the mission school they were something of an embarrassment to her with their bleached blondness, their whiteness through-and-through. Alice Fay was dark like the others, an Indian child. She belonged in an Indian school. When the other children saw Norma and

Tilly and realized who they were, they could see Alice Fay was unlike them. "White girl," they would sneer at her. "White girl, we ain't got no use for you." Let them forget she was a white girl. She herself would do her best to forget.

It was around this time Alice Fay became an atheist. She knew Brides of Jesus could not be as mean as the nuns she knew (Jesus would just divorce them so fast it would make their heads spin if they were). And God, if He existed, didn't give a damn about her. He didn't give a damn about anyone, no matter what they thought. It made people feel better to imagine some big God up in the sky over them all, who always had everyone's best interests at heart even when it looked like He didn't, who worked in such strange ways that everything made some sort of sense even though nobody could see it. They got along better that way, deluding themselves, like characters in cartoons that can run on air until they realize there's nothing beneath their feet. People believed in Him because it suited them to do so. Alice Fay did not believe for the same reason. She could accept the indifference of the universe more easily than she could a cruel God or a God that works in such destructive ways his wonders to perform.

Gradually, as the years passed, Alice Fay adjusted to her bleak existence. She even thought of becoming a nun herself, not that she heard a calling or anything (and she guessed that none, or almost none, heard a calling). If she could "take the veil" and live in a cloister, then she would

◄○►
Alice Fay

never have to go out on her own. She would have peace and quiet, a neat, austere, ordered existence, and not be bothered. Who would ever guess she didn't believe in God?

When Alice Fay opened the door, Aunt Tilly uncharacteristically threw her arms around her and hugged her close. "How's my little niece this beautiful morning?" she said up close. So early yet her breath smelled of alcohol and cigarettes and perfume and some sort of mint meant to cover up. She wore perfume much more sophisticated and costly than Norma's floral scents. Tilly liked perfume from the Far East. This one seemed cedar-like.

"I'm fine, Aunt Tilly, how about yourself?" Tilly, in black corduroy toreador pants tucked in gold lamé boots, black turtleneck under her old, poor-quality, short-haired mink coat, looked like a dyed and powdered, over-the-hill tart. Alice Fay wondered if she had always done herself up this way. It didn't seem so. Alice Fay remembered her as she remembered Norma, glamorous beyond words.

"How am I you ask? Don't ask. Believe me you don't want to know. I've about had it with Karl. Be a dear and bring me a glass of sherry," she said, heading toward Norma's room.

"It's waiting for you," Alice Fay said.

Twenty minutes later Alice Fay slipped out of the apartment with the dirty laundry without telling the sisters good-bye. They were deeply lost in conversation and sherry (which Norma, of course, was not supposed to have; Alice Fay let her have it because, as Norma put it, sherry was one of the few pleasures of her life).

Today she decided not to do the laundry at the place down the street. Instead she put it in her car and drove to a pretty, picturesque district in the dirty little industrial city. This laundromat had an attendant who played classical music on the radio and made free coffee for the customers.

Alice Fay had to wait for a machine, but she didn't mind. She sat on an easy chair and listened to the soothing music and drank the rich, fragrant free coffee someone else had made and read articles in the magazines provided by the management. When one machine became available (it seemed the place was frequented by single people with only one tub of laundry to do) she put two loads into it, light and dark together. Then she went away for awhile. She looked in store windows, browsed in a bookstore, considered taking in a film at the little neighborhood theater: *A Man and a Woman,* the marquee said. She had lunch at a Greek restaurant that played music reminiscent of *Zorba the Greek.* She didn't even try to hurry herself.

When she got back to the laundromat a long while later, some irate person had taken out her laundry and thrown it on the floor. She glanced at the attendant, who didn't look up from her book. She washed it all again (this time in two tubs, properly, as she should have done in the first place).

By the time she backed into a parking space in front and across the street from their building, the winter sun had set. She looked up at their apartment window, which looked out over this street, and saw no light. There would be hell to pay now, she thought. Well, she could take it.

Tilly was gone and the apartment was dark except for the light of the TV in Norma's room. Norma didn't call to her, which was unusual. Maybe, Alice Fay thought, Norma got drunk on sherry and passed out. It had happened before. Alice Fay went about her business then and did not disturb her mother. At ten o'clock, uneasily, Alice Fay looked in on Norma and found her dead.

The ten o'clock news had just begun: wars and floods and snow and ice. Up in the mountain pass three cars had been buried in an avalanche. The bank robbers who didn't get away the day before and kept hostages had given themselves up after twenty hours. A murder-suicide in Renton. On the lighter side, someone had found someone else's lost pet boa constrictor. The finder had noticed the boa peeking at her from the heat vent as she sat in the bathtub.

Alice Fay looked down at her mother's dead face in the flickering light. Her unseeing eyes stared at the ceiling. Even in the dim, uneven TV light she could see Norma (or now the corpse) wore lipstick and eyebrow pencil. Tilly must have made her up. Norma sometimes made herself up, but it was a painstaking process and never turned out this neat and even. Maybe this time it had.

Alice Fay reached down and felt Norma's neck for a pulse; the old woman's flesh was cold. Alice Fay closed the blank eyes and sat down in the hardly-ever-used wheelchair beside Norma's bed. Cold weather headed our way, the TV said, such as Tacoma hardly ever experiences. Odd, Alice Fay thought, that Norma would die like this. She had, with dread, imagined Norma would last another ten years, becoming more and more helpless and demanding and then, it would be a drawn-out death with tubes and IVs and breathing machines and weeks in intensive care. But it was like this: quick and easy when Alice Fay was not even there.

Alice Fay

Aunt Tilly, not Alice Fay, was beneficiary of Norma's $30,000 policy, which did not surprise Alice Fay, though she hoped it would turn out Norma had named her own daughter (she did leave her one dollar to show she hadn't forgotten her). Tilly told Alice Fay she could keep the two-year-old TV set Norma had paid for. Tilly took charge of all the funeral arrangements.

Her sister deserved the very best, Tilly said, the very best. Norma's army widow benefits would pay for a funeral. Tilly decided to have Norma cremated, not, she said, because of the lower cost, but because Norma, when she was a little girl, used to have nightmares about being buried alive in the ground. And she had said to Tilly, or so Tilly said, "Promise me, if I die first you'll have me cremated and my ashes scattered over the Pacific Ocean." Now Tilly meant to honor that request. It seemed an unlikely request for a child to have made, especially the detail of scattering the ashes over the *Pacific* (not the Atlantic or Indian or any other ocean). Alice Fay didn't care one way or another. Tilly was free to do as she liked.

Not many people came to the funeral mass besides Tilly and Alice Fay. Karl, Tilly's current boyfriend, who wore a hearing aid and didn't seem, most of the time, to know what was going on around him, slumped over the pew before the service began and fell asleep. All the way through he snored lightly. A couple of neighbors from their building came and so did Norma's aide, Mariann, and Agnes, Alice Fay's best friend from the DMV, who told her she had to leave as soon as the service was over and return to work, but would visit that evening and the two would have dinner together in Alice Fay's (*only* Alice Fay's now) apartment.

About midway through the service, when the priest had just said something about life not ending, only being transformed, Alice Fay, for some reason, turned and looked to the back of the church. She saw an old Indian man sitting there and, even before she was told who he was, she remembered thinking to herself that he had a kind-looking, weathered face.

"Who is that?" she nudged her aunt, who was dabbing her eyes with a pretty, feminine handkerchief with lace edging, careful not to smudge her eyeliner or mascara.

Tilly turned and looked, squinting her eyes. "I think that's your father," she whispered, and resumed dabbing her eyes.

"My father?" Her father?

Alice Fay kept her eyes trained straight ahead for the rest of the service. Though she wanted to look again, she dared not. What if he wasn't there? She couldn't hear the priest anymore or think of anything except she was going to see her father, at long last. She'd dreamed of that moment so many times in childhood.

The priest said something about Norma being a servant of God whom He had commanded to His side. And then something about how Norma would live on in the hearts of her beloved sister and beloved daughter.

Alice Fay thought of how Norma had looked, Norma's corpse that is, in the "slumber room" of the mortuary: the bloom of health artificially restored to her face, her peaceful expression, her long grey hair blonde again (most likely specially ordered by Tilly), her turquoise-blue silk dress that had been one of Tilly's wedding outfits. Her mother was beautiful again, just as she was in Alice Fay's old memories.

Norma's remains had already been cremated. Alice Fay dimly remembered something about the church not approving of cremations. Alice Fay didn't know what Tilly told the priest regarding the absence of a corpse. Sometime soon, she didn't know when, the Neptune Society would take Norma's ashes (and, presumably, those of others) up in a little airplane and scatter them over Puget Sound.

When it was time to leave, Tilly put her handkerchief away. Karl woke up. Alice Fay stood up and turned and looked to the rear of the church. Her father was gone. Was a glimpse all she would ever have of him?

She found him waiting on the front steps of the church. He wasn't as he'd been in her childhood fantasies: He was neither handsome nor dashing and certainly not rich. He wore rather shabby clothes and a black patch over his left eye and was a good deal older than she thought he'd be, much older than Norma. Alice Fay felt dizzy. Incense always did that to her.

"I'm your father, Sarah," the old man said, and Alice Fay's heart skipped a beat. Her father! "My name is Joe," he extended his hand, which was a big, heavily-veined working man's hand. She took it and felt the rough calluses. "How do you do?"

Father and daughter shook hands. Joe, holding his hat, looked down at the church steps. "I'd like to take you for some ice cream. That is, if you don't mind. You don't have to."

"Okay," she said. "There's an ice cream store just down the street."

Joe wasn't much of a talker and neither was Alice Fay. They ate their banana splits in silence. They were the only ones there, except for the high school boy behind the counter, because it was a chilly late-December day, not a time when ice cream stores did a lot of business.

Do I look like him? she wondered studying his face. His features were large, craggy, whereas hers were small, and his nose had been broken more than once. Everyone who knew she and Norma were mother and daughter always remarked on how unlike they were. Most likely she did look like Joe; she had to look like someone. She imagined that people on the street passing the ice cream store might look in the window and see them and remark, "Look at that woman and her father sitting in there eating ice cream on a cold day like this!" Everyone would know they were father and daughter. Everyone could tell.

"How's your ice cream?" Joe asked.

"Good. How's yours?"

"Good. Real good. It hits the spot."

When they finished they walked the block and a half back to St. Anthony's then parted company in the church parking lot. His vehicle was an old black pickup with Idaho plates. Hers was a grey Volkswagen that had seen better days.

"Here's my address," Joe said just before she got into her car, taking a folded piece of paper out of his jacket pocket and handing it to her. "You can write to me anytime you feel like it." She took the paper and put it in her purse.

"Thanks, Joe. Thank you for coming. I'm glad you came. Good-bye."

"Good-bye, Sarah," he said calling her again by the name he'd given her when she was born, which Granny Gloria hadn't liked. Sarah. A good name. Strong. Not frivolous.

At home Alice Fay flew into a frenzy of cleaning and reordering. Norma had left a lot behind. At around seven Agnes called and said she wouldn't be able to make it for dinner after all. Her own parents had shown up unexpectedly (they lived in Kansas). But next week they would go out and have dinner in a nice restaurant, Agnes' treat, and take in a movie. Sure, Alice Fay said, whatever. Now she had to get back to the work she'd begun.

She worked into the night making trip after trip to the garbage chute with Norma's things. She knew she was being wasteful and ought to instead give them to St. Vincent de Paul or Catholic Charities or even the Salvation Army, but, now that she'd begun, she wanted very badly to get this reordering over and done with.

Norma had had many glamour-puss photos taken of herself over the years and saved all of them (none of her wedding pictures, however, not even the last one of her and the retired army colonel that did not end in divorce), but none of her daughter. Alice Fay saved one cheesecake picture of Norma at about age eighteen: she was wearing shorts and a halter and was sitting on the hood of a car. Alice Fay put the rest away to give to Tilly. She moved Norma's hospital bed and wheelchair out of the room, then scrubbed down the floor and walls and moved herself into that larger, lighter, better room and stored the hospital bed and wheelchair in what had been her room. Later she would try to sell them. They must be worth something secondhand. They had cost a lot new. She decided to keep the case and a half of sherry. Though she wasn't much of a drinker, she did like sherry. That night she slept in her new room and dreamed she was a little girl at St. Jude's Mission School and her father came to get her and bring her home with him. She woke up weeping and realized she had not wept, not a single tear, for Norma.

When she returned to her job at the DMV the next day, her supervisor informed her she had accumulated sixty days of vacation and she would lose it all unless she took it now. She had never had a vacation. Okay, she said, no problem. She would take a vacation. Lord knows she could use one.

"Go to Hawaii!" Agnes said. Alice Fay could not do that since she had little saved up. She couldn't see herself in Hawaii somehow. She bet it was touristy.

"Then go to Mexico," Agnes said. No, no, no. She reminded Agnes of the Mexican men who hooted at them from cars when they walked down the street. Mexican men in this country did not respect women; what would they be like in Mexico? How would they treat an American woman traveling alone? Mexico was out. Maybe Alaska. She had been thinking of Alaska. The idea of Alaska was exciting. America's last frontier. That would be an adventure.

"Alaska? Alice, are you out of your mind?"

"Maybe. I don't think so. I heard there's lots of men in Alaska."

"There are men *here*."

"True. But they're so boring, and the odds are better in the Land of the Midnight Sun; ten men for every woman."

"What would you do with ten men? And besides, you know it's cold in Alaska. Real cold."

"Yeah. So?"

"So I don't care. It's your vacation. Go head on! Go to Alaska and freeze your butt off." Alice Fay imagined herself in Alaska, smiling face framed in fur (the hood of her parka would be trimmed in fur) turned up to the sky, snow lightly falling, a few flakes catching on her lashes before they melted.

That night she had what she thought was going to be an erotic dream, but this time, instead of Charles Bronson, Paul Newman showed up at their rendezvous, grinning his winning grin, his too-pale blue eyes in his suntanned face sparkling. Well, he had appeal, but he was no Charles Bronson. She didn't say anything but she thought, "What the hell is going on here. Could Charles not make it so he sent this bozo in his place? What kind of bullshit is this?" As if reading her mind, Paul winked and then faded into thin air, like a ghost. This startled her and she woke and couldn't get back to sleep.

The next day she wrote a letter to her father. *"Dear Dad,"* she began. Then stopped to look at the words, to savor the moment. She had never before addressed anyone by "Dad" or "Daddy" or "Papa" or "Father" or "Mother" or "Mum" or "Mamma." It felt strange to do so. She began writing.

I'm not sorry my mother died. Does that shock you? She was a miserable nuisance (that's what she used to tell me when I was little. I had a miserable childhood, Dad). What I feel sorry about is that Tilly, not me, was her beneficiary. Tilly hit the jackpot and won $30,000. I'm the one who looked after her, bathed her, cooked her meals, washed her clothes, listened to her whine. I got nothing for my time and effort but a stupid case of sherry.

And you know something? Now that she's gone, I feel empty. I don't know what to do with myself. Is this how the slaves felt when they were emancipated at last? At loose ends? Not knowing which way to turn? Did they fantasize about running away to Alaska? What would I have done with $30,000? Maybe I'd move to a city more glamorous than Tacoma. San Francisco, maybe. I'd take a cruise around the world. I'd buy myself another Volkswagen.

When I was younger I wanted very much to see the world, beginning with Paris, France. When I was a teenager in a government boarding school in Oklahoma,

Alice Fay

my best friend and I planned a trip to Europe. We went to a travel agency and got brochures and we opened a savings account and got all the baby-sitting and house and yard cleaning jobs we could find. Our bank account grew. We dreamed of Paris, of Rome, of London, of romance. We deeply regretted that our school did not offer courses in any foreign languages (only vocational training courses). But we were poor girls. Winter came and there we were in our worn, out-of-style, cheap coats. The bank account was there. We didn't discuss it much. We got into it and bought ourselves beautiful, warm winter coats, exactly alike. They were forest green with gold satin lining and luxurious fur collars. That was the end of the trip to Europe.

I'm too old for Europe now (as you know, or maybe don't remember, I'll be thirty-one years old in just three days). The thought of traveling to Europe fills me with anxiety. I'm too old now for romance, too.

Dad, where were you when I was growing up? I was in mission school and wicked BIA schools and was sorely mistreated until I learned to blend in, until I deliberately made myself become institutionalized. I was so lonely, Dad. Nobody ever told me anything about you. After so many years without your trying to make contact, I assumed you were dead.

Norma wouldn't even let me call her
mother. She was ashamed of me because
I'm such a darkie. Why didn't you come for
me, Dad? Where were you?

She mailed the letter not expecting a reply. It was
rather accusatory, after all. And whining. Maybe
even self-pitying.

Alice Fay didn't go anywhere on her vacation.
She drank sherry and listened to the radio and
read movie magazines. She lost track of time and
didn't even realize it was her birthday the day
she turned thirty-one. She didn't go to Alaska,
but Alaska came to her.

Tacoma froze as never before and immobilized
the dark, drab little city and covered it over. It fell
so deep you couldn't see the tops of the parking
meters or even the cars parked at them. Bus lines
did not run and schools closed down until fur-
ther notice. This was what she wanted. She
hoped the snow would continue to fall until her
entire apartment building was covered in it, until
she, along with the rest of the city, was buried in
snow. She broke out another bottle of sherry to
celebrate the ice and snow.

To conserve heat she closed off her new bedroom and moved herself into the living room and
made herself a bed on the sofa. This was better,
she thought. The back of the sofa made her feel
as though she were being cradled in someone's
soft, strong arms. And she could sit up and lean
her elbows on the top of the back of the sofa,

which was covered in maroon or burgundy-colored velvet, and look out over the street below. She finished one bottle of sherry and opened another. She turned on the radio and tuned in to the station that played music from the '30s and '40s. Norma and Joe were young when this music was new, she thought.

She only ate when she had to and then only a baked potato or TV dinner. She could feel herself growing thinner, or anyway, less plump. When she returned to work, everyone would tell her she looked great. All the women would be so jealous of her weight loss.

Joe's letter arrived. She didn't open it for a day or two. She kept it on the sill of the window behind the sofa. Sometimes she would pick up the envelope in the night when she lay unable to sleep and whisper to it, "Where were you, Joe? Where were you?"

It was night when she at last opened her letter and read it by the light from the street lamp. Billie Holiday sang "Trav'lin' Light" on the radio. The signal was not strong and her voice sounded faint and very far away, as it really was.

The snow fell, not hard anymore, but lightly. She was a little drunk, as she usually was now. She wasn't used to all that drinking.

"Dear Daughter," his letter began. There was something else; a check for a thousand dollars and it was made out to Sarah Whitehawk. What must a thousand dollars mean to a man as poor as Joe? Why did he send it? She read on.

I am very sorry I neglected you when you
were a kid, and though there is no excuse, I
hope you will forgive me. I thought of you a
lot, Sarah. Every January on your birthday
I remembered you and tried to imagine
what you must look like as each year
passed and I hoped you were happy. For all
I knew, Norma got married to some man
with money. A woman with her looks
could get herself a well-to-do husband. And
maybe your stepfather was very good to
you and the three of you made a happy
family. I did not want to intrude. Besides, I
was not my usual self for a long while after
Norma left me. I was dead inside. I used to
drink a lot, a whole lot, so much I would
lose days, get put in jail, all kinds of things.
Then I started to straighten up, I got remar-
ried myself about fifteen years back, but my
wife, she died. I've got a boy now I'm
raising alone. We do okay. He's a good boy.
Enclosed please find a check made out to
you for one-thousand dollars. I know it
can't make up to you for the years of
neglect. Neither am I trying to buy you off
or anything. I know it won't pay for a trip
to Europe, but I also know you can
probably use the money. Buy yourself
another good winter coat like the one you
bought when you were a teenager in
Oklahoma. Buy some nice kid gloves and a
scarf and boots. The works. If you want,

Alice Fay

daughter, you can come visit me. You're always welcome.

With all my love, your dad, Joe

Alice Fay opened the window behind and over the sofa. She didn't realize until that moment how stale the air inside the apartment was and that she hadn't breathed fresh air in a long time. She raised the comforter up over her head and rested her chin on the sofa, looking out, breathing in the cold air as a few snowflakes blew in and gently melted on her face.

Snow, fine and dry, quickly gathered on the sill and against the back of the sofa. Billie Holiday's voice had completely drifted away, and all that could be heard on the radio was static, faint and distant.

—◄○►—

Deborah and Her Snakes (A Cautionary Tale)

A woman I know, Deborah is her name, (actually she's a distant relative) told me this story.

In the dead of last winter, an odd dream kept recurring: a white snake would appear to her. She found him repulsive, as she had an aversion to snakes, yet, at the same time he was cute. More than cute. Alluring.

"Follow me," he said. "Come. Follow me." And she obeyed, following him over rolling hills and fields, into thick woodsy woods, even, sometimes, having to wade through streams.

Every so often the white snake would go into a hole in the ground then appear somewhere in the distance and it was for her to spy him, then he would signal her, motioning with his head, "Come on. Let's go."

Now this woman, a single mother of four, had had a serious illness of long duration finally requiring major surgery. As a result of her illness she lost her job, which had paid just enough to keep her and her children going from one paycheck to the next.

She had pawned or sold what she could: her camera, her microwave, her suede jacket, and finally her television set. A gold brooch she'd inherited from her grandmother would be next. She was penniless or at least dollarless.

One morning she woke from a white snake dream, got her three oldest children off to school, then bundled up her youngest daughter and herself, got into her old rattletrap one-eyed Ford, and drove ten miles over winding, icy roads to the food bank. The one-eyed Ford shook, coughed, and strained all the way.

The food bank gave her a cardboard carton containing powdered milk and eggs, frozen elk meat, bags of pasta, rice, beans, and cans of fruit and vegetables, for which she was very grateful.

On the way home the Ford's heater went out and the windows fogged over then turned to ice. Finally, mercifully, halfway home the engine died never, she knew, to start again.

She got out of the car and set both her daughter and box of food upon the hood and closed the door. Then, carrying her daughter on her shoulders and the box in her arms, she set off walking toward home.

Soon a familiar magenta jeep stopped. The owner was an old woman she knew (a relative of some sort) who lived not far from her in the same village. She told the old woman her tale of woe nearly, but not quite, shedding a tear when she got to the part about the washing machine breaking down.

"Look to your dreams, young woman," her neighbor and distant relative advised. "A person should always pay attention to her dreams.

Especially in times of urgent need." So she told the old woman about her odd white snake dreams.

"White snake! Oh my word! Gambler's patron. The Good Luck Snake. Good luck will be yours! I'll come by for you tomorrow night and I'll lend you the $20 you'll need to play high-stakes bingo. The white snake has chosen you, you lucky girl you. You'll win big."

We all know how it went that night: The white snake was her salvation. She won $10,000 and suddenly her lights were no longer in danger of being shut off. Her phone was turned on again. She bought a good used car and studded snow tires for it and a color TV and a satellite dish. She bought new winter coats for all of them. She lived frugally and had enough to live on without having to revisit the food bank. In the spring she found a job far better than the one she'd had before.

So you could say this story had a happy ending. But still, in the dead of winter just a few nights after her big win, another snake, a sinister, ugly one, visited her in a dream.

She told the woman who owned the magenta jeep, "This awful red snake slithered out of the tall grass and across my back yard, climbed the tree that grows near my bedroom window, and wound around a branch. He peered right in at me. I tried to get away but was unable to move. He called my name: 'Deborah,' he said, 'Deborah. Where does my Deborah be?' I couldn't get up but I could close my eyes. I didn't have to look at that weird creature but I did have to hear it.

'Don't follow me, Deborah, whose real name is She-Who-Belongs-To-Me. Don't follow. You know it's not wise. Don't follow. If you can!'

"The dark side of gambling," the old woman said. "That is what the red one is. I should have warned you before. If you pursue gambling, my dear, the red snake is what you'll get. If you gamble you have to accept the red snake who brings only ruin!"

But, Deborah said, she didn't need to be warned. She knew what everyone knew: to gamble is, ultimately, to lose. In the end nobody wins. Except the house, that is.

A young man, a tribal member, had met with a bad end. His wife had thrown him out for gambling away his whole paycheck (again) at the bingo casino. He worked at a warehouse and took to sleeping there. He went to the casino when he got his next paycheck. The wildfire jackpot was way up there, more than thirty grand. He blew his whole check on the wildfire machines. He was in good spirits, the casino workers said, his old self, in fact, smiling, joking away.

He maxed out his credit cards. Then he took all the cash out of his and his wife's joint account (did I mention he was the father of two young children?). When that was gone, around three A.M., he left.

My next door neighbor, who works at the warehouse where the gambler worked, found him around eight A.M. hanging from the rafters. Not a pretty sight.

Then, of course, there's Peggy Sue, a grand-mother who had had a responsible job with the tribe for many years, a job that involved handling large amounts of money. Peggy Sue, who had a spotless record, embezzled money, many thousands of dollars, before anyone caught on. And now there she sits in the women's house of correction.

My relative Deborah and I both saw Gladys Knight (without the Pips) on TV hawking a book she'd written. She said she hit rock bottom when she lost $14,000 at one sitting. Then she joined Gambler's Anonymous and now works the same twelve steps over and over again.

Deborah said she was too smart to get suckered in. She knew how to walk away a winner. But, not long after she told me her story, on a balmy summer night, I saw her at the casino. I saw her, her cheeks red as in fever, her eyes glassy-bright and crazy-looking in their intensity, sitting at the Mighty Buffalo slots. She saw me, I'm sure, as I saw her, but she acknowledged me not.

I saw her feed bill after bill into her machine, without a return, $20, $40, $80. Four-hundred dollars in less than an hour's time. Then she walked quickly past, cheeks red and eyes shining, and went out the front door.

You've got to watch out for those snakes. They will seduce you with initial good luck and promises of big wins, trying to make you believe, against all reason, that you're the lucky one.

White Snake/Red Snake. They want your soul. Once they get ahold of you, they never let you go. Red Snake/White Snake. Some say they're in cahoots. Others say they're one in the same.

Alma

Alma didn't even try not to blame herself for getting pregnant just when it seemed the long period of poverty and deprivation was over. *Stupid,* she said to herself. *Stupid.*

Alma and her four-year-old son James had moved from the roach-infested apartment in a San Francisco slum to a new, clean, boxy little apartment in Student Family Housing in Berkeley. They would have enough combined income from her work-study job, her federal loan, and a generous grant (a gift to the university for an Indian woman student entering from a California community college with advanced standing who had a GPA of at least 3.5) for James and her to live on. She had bought a wreck of a car ("good transportation" the ad in the student paper had said) for $80. She'd bought them both new shoes and new clothes, a tricycle for James, a typewriter for her, and textbooks, pens, spiral notebooks. All through her first year of college she could buy no books. She was not the only student at City College who was that poor. There were always copies of required texts on reserve in the library, and she studied all she could, but one was not allowed to remove these from the library.

Now she could study at home, at her leisure. Those "welfare mother living in the slums going without eating" days were in the past.

And then a Chicano woman named Maria Elena, who was in her American Institutions class (they were currently studying the transcripts from the Sacco-Vanzetti trial) and to whom she had spoken a time or two, invited Alma to a party.

It was that she had to work so hard all the time, she told herself, count her pennies, make sure James' needs were taken care of, be ever vigilant. She had been a poor, teen-aged welfare mother with an eighth-grade education and had never even set foot inside a high school. She had beaten the odds to get as far as she was. Beat the hell out of the odds and was proud of herself for that.

Her existence had been bleak, but not sad. She never despaired except for brief periods, when she had to miss a day of eating and hunger pangs kept her awake at night and she had to be up early and maybe she had just one dollar left and five days to go to the first of the month (welfare check day) and each bus ride cost fifteen cents. At those times she would wonder if she were deluding herself. Maybe she was not college material. Maybe she couldn't really be almost anything she wanted to be. What then? But she always got over these attacks. James and Alma got by. The day-care center gave him hot, balanced breakfasts and lunches and afternoon snacks. He never had to go a whole day without eating. And, thanks partly to the daycare center, where she paid a truly paltry sum, he was growing up, in spite of their circumstances, strong and healthy. And now he even had his own tricycle.

She'd begun to think about a master's in public health. A master's degree in public health was something only other people got (like her academic advisor, for instance, or the single mother, Cyn, who lived in the apartment directly below hers with her baby girl Thomasina). Maybe she'd casually said it to one or two classmates, trying it out to see how it felt. Actually, though, she had something else on her mind. A big dream, one she didn't want to share with anyone yet, not until other people could see it as a possibility: Alma wanted to become a doctor of medicine.

The year before she started college, when James was a toddler and she was eighteen, she went to the University Medical Center in San Francisco looking for work. The medical center had put an ad in the classifieds: clerk typists wanted. Alma knew she wasn't a good typist, but maybe she would pick up enough speed. It couldn't hurt anything to apply.

After she filled out a form and gave it back to the receptionist, she was told to take a seat in another waiting room that adjoined the larger one they were in. The main room was full. She did as she was told. A group of young people, mostly men, some wearing white coats and pants, waited in this room. An older man wearing a doctor's ID pin came into the room and told them to come along and follow him. All of them, including Alma, got up and followed him down the hall and down another hall and down the stairs and into a laboratory.

"This experiment will last eight weeks," the doctor told the group of young people, "and you will be paid the usual fee. I will need you three afternoons a week for two hours. If you have classes that conflict with this, or if for any reason you can't come in the afternoons, you may leave." Three of the students left the room. Alma realized they were medical students and the doctor had mistaken her for one, too, and none of the real medical students seemed to realize she was not one of them.

Her ex-husband Lennie, Lennie the pot head, Lennie the wife beater, would have ridiculed her if he knew she was thinking *this is how it would feel to be a medical student, someone with a future, with aspirations.* She *was* good enough to be a medical student, just look at her! They all thought she was a bright young woman who would one day soon be a physician, healing the sick and injured, saving people's lives. They could not tell, just by looking at her, that she was just a poor girl, an orphan, a former battered wife who had had to quit her job at the post office because she couldn't find a sitter when her hours were changed to graveyard. And, unless she was able to find a decent job, she and James both were about to become "welfare bums" (as the governor of California referred to welfare recipients). She would cherish that magical moment that allowed her to know how it felt to be a respected member of society before she said she was applying for a job and waiting for an interview and had been swept along by mistake. She didn't believe it was a mistake, really. It was the incident that made her decide she would attempt to go to college. And maybe someday go to medical school. She had successfully completed a year of college and that was very rewarding, but she had had to work so hard without letting up, almost without recreation of any kind. She needed to relax and socialize and have some fun. That was why, she reasoned later, she'd overindulged at Maria Elena's party. She hadn't been having a good time there before the man with the beard showed up. She had looked forward to attending, to being among people, other students who were near her own age. She'd made up her face and bought a beautiful white blouse to wear to this wine-drinking, pot-smoking party where she was ignored. She didn't know what she'd expected, but knew it wasn't this.

Most of her fellow partygoers were Chicano and they jabbered away to one another in Spanish. Alma emptied her wine glass and thought *How rude!* and *No wonder they have to live in barrios in LA.* Next time she would know better. She poured herself another glass of cheap, awful-tasting wine, swallowed it, and soon felt all right, no longer bothered by the jabbering or the fact that she was being left out. Let them leave her out! The wine made her feel light-hearted, and young. Though she was only twenty, she hadn't felt young in a long, long time, and then she was dancing with a shaggy-haired, bearded man she'd never seen before. He wasn't a student. He was much older than any other person there. Thirty, thirty-two or -three. Something like that. He spoke English to her; he spoke nonsense telling her how beautiful she was. She looked like an Aztec princess, he said. She laughed. How did he know how an Aztec princess looked? "I know," he said, "I know. Never mind how."

She laughed and danced the cha-cha and was young for a night. She drank so much that when she woke up the next morning with a dry mouth and a pounding headache beside the man she had been dancing with, she could only vaguely remember the sex they'd had. She dressed and crept quietly to the door, trying not to wake him, but, just as she touched the door knob, and glanced over her shoulder at him, he opened his eyes, the whites of which were all bloodshot. He smiled slightly. He badly needed a shave.

She remembered he'd had slightly crooked front teeth, which were easy to overlook last night. She couldn't remember his name. Pedro? Jose? Jesus. In Spanish, "Hey, Seuss." She remembered the others addressing him as "Seuss" or they'd say, "Hey, Seuss!" and she'd thought he must have been named after the famous author of *Cat in the Hat*, Doctor Seuss. She hoped he didn't remember her name. She felt ashamed of herself. She hoped she never saw him again, hoped he wouldn't ask for her phone number or anything. He said, "Good morning. Are you leaving?"

"Yes."

"Oh. Good-bye. Have a good life."

"Adios," she told him and opened his bedroom door and left through his small apartment and out the front. She would just forget that stupid night, she thought, put it behind her. Three weeks later she began having what she recognized as morning sickness and three weeks after that went to planned parenthood where they confirmed her pregnancy.

She went to Mexico City, which was much farther away than she supposed it was and the altitude so high her nose bled off and on the whole time she was there.

The abortion was quick, and it was safe, of this she was sure. She was glad she hadn't gone to Tijuana, which was cheaper and closer, but she'd heard such horror stories of abortions gone wrong in Tijuana, of women bleeding to death or dying due to blood poisoning or being rendered sterile or returning home after an abortion only to find out, too late, that they were still pregnant and giving birth to damaged babies, the result of botched abortions—one little girl with an eye that didn't work and hideous scarring around it and a little boy born with one arm missing, cut from his shoulder when he was a tiny fetus by a Tijuana abortionist.

In Mexico City, the doctor's clinic was in his home, which was a mansion the likes of which Alma had never seen. It was built of adobe with a red tile roof, and behind a great stone wall with a high iron gate. The grounds were beautifully kept. The clinic was very clean, the room looked like a hospital operating room, and two nurses, both middle-aged with kind, overly made-up faces, assisted the doctor. The doctor was courteous, even friendly, asking her, "¿Habla español, señorita?" He thought she was Mexican American. They all did, it seemed, in Mexico City. She was already under the drug— what was it? Sodium penathol, maybe. It didn't knock her out, just dazed her, just made her less vulnerable to pain, and it made her feel as though she were floating rather like the near-death experiences she'd read about when the soul of the dead, or near-dead person, leaves the body and floats up, hovering above and observing everything that's done to the body, hearing every word spoken. "¿Habla español, señorita?" the nice doctor asked. She knew a little Spanish she'd learned in a class last year at City College before it proved too great a struggle with no textbook and having to attend every day or fall behind. She couldn't afford not to get a high mark in every course she took. Her escape, her ticket out of poverty and ignorance depended upon it, so she'd dropped out.

"¿Habla español, señorita?" the doctor who stood over her as she lay with thighs spread, feet in metal stirrups on his operating table asked. It was so cold in that room.

"Lo siento mucho," she answered the doctor, floating in air, "pero no." (*I'm very sorry, but no.*) The doctor and nurses chuckled. She supposed it was because she hadn't just said "No." There wasn't a lot of pain, only a little, and because of the drug she couldn't even fight against the intrusion. Her body just accepted it, let itself be forced open and scraped out. She'd had a wisdom tooth pulled not long ago. The abortion was less painful and took less time. And there she was. Pregnant no more!

Back at the hotel Alma could not rest. And, since she hadn't slept well the night before, she was tired, very tired. Sometimes, when she felt anxious she would take a long, hot bath, but Doctor Rodriquez had told her no baths for at least two weeks. She took a hot shower that did not help.

The anxiety mounted; she didn't know why. She had never experienced anything like it. *This must be what they call a panic attack.* She could feel her pulse racing. She paced back and forth from one wall to the other and back again. The abortion was over and done with, shouldn't she feel relief? Anxiety is, or seems to be a form of fear, but fear is something that can be dealt with: Separate yourself from whatever threatens you and everything will be okay. Get away from the husband who would harm you, who would, he said, *kill* you. Work your way out of poverty.

Don't have a baby that would pull you back down into poverty. Have it taken out of your body and then forget it. Let it be as though there had never been anything there. Anxiety was a lot like fear. What was there to be afraid of? Maybe she was just having an adverse reaction to the drugs she'd been given. Or maybe it was the altitude. It didn't matter *what* it was. It was painful. What would happen to her if it didn't go away? She turned on the television and all that was on, on all of the channels, was the funeral of the president of Mexico. His casket, draped with the flag of Mexico, was being transported through the streets in an open horse-drawn wagon. Crowds of people stood on either side of the street to watch him pass. He must have been a beloved leader. People would not turn out like that for the funeral of a dictator, would they? Later on there'd be soap operas. Everything in Spanish.

Alma pictured the pull-down map of the world in sixth grade. She used to study it and study it and imagine going to the places shown on the map: The Yukon, Siberia, Bombay, Nairobi, Rio de Janeiro, Moscow (not the Moscow in Idaho near the reservation—she'd been there often enough), Russia on the other side of the world; Down Under (except, when she grew up and sent for immigration papers to go to Australia she found that the government wanted only people of "European descent" to immigrate there). She presumed they meant by that "white people," not, say, a black person with an Irish great-grandfather or herself, an American Indian with a Scottish great-great-great grandfather, which made her, technically "of European descent." But not white. Why didn't Australia just come right out and say they didn't want anyone who wasn't white and who were they anyway to say that? Just a bunch of descendants of European criminals was all they were, and they, the descendants of criminals, treated their aboriginal people so shabbily. She imagined Moscow, Idaho on the map of the world, then San Francisco, the place she ran to. And here, where she was this very minute, Mexico City. She was far, far from home and everything familiar.

Alma's mother died when she was just six and then her father married a Gorgon (hideous one). She'd never understood why he married a woman at least a decade older than he. Surely he hadn't "fallen in love." And then her father died when Alma was twelve, leaving her to deal with the Gorgon as best she could, which meant getting away. She got away when she was just fifteen and she never looked back. Her sister Marta escaped the Gorgon before Alma did by marrying a man much older than herself and having babies right away. Alma didn't even know how many Marta had before she was through. Maybe she wasn't even through yet. Alma never wrote one letter home. She'd lost her sister in those years of silence. She could use a sister, a big sister, now. She could use a mother, a mom. She still remembered perfectly the sound of her mother's voice.

Oh, if she could hear her mother's voice just one more time. She was a motherless child a long time. In some part of her soul she would always be a motherless child.

"*Pray to the Blessed Virgin Mary,*" she almost heard her mother say.

"*Pray to the Blessed Virgin,*" her Catholic mother said again. Of course her mother couldn't know that Alma was an atheist or at the very least an agnostic, a very cynical agnostic who could never believe in such things as the ascension of the Blessed Virgin or that certain saints should be prayed to so that they would influence God to answer your prayers. (As if God didn't have a mind of his own.)

Alma answered the voice she imagined, "I can't pray to the Virgin Mary, Mother. Don't you know the stand of the Catholic Church on abortion?"

"And who is 'The Catholic Church'? The Pope. And is the Pope God or even a saint? He is not. He's nothing but a weird old man running around the Vatican in fancy robes, receiving visitors who kiss his ring. He sits and passes judgment on what he can know nothing about. 'No birth control,' he tells all the poor women the world over who can scarcely feed and clothe the children they have. Who is the Pope to tell them no birth control? I bet he'd change his mind in a hurry if *he* had to go through a pregnancy, vomiting and a big swollen belly and water retention in his feet and ankles. If *he* had to suffer labor pains that feel as though a dozen demons from hell had hold of him, if he had to change dirty diapers, et cetera. You get my point. No birth control. No divorce. What a power trip.

"But the Blessed Virgin Mary will understand. Mary was a woman, a mortal woman just like you and me. And, a *poor* one! She understands the worries and hardships we endure. She knows all about them. Pray to her, the holy mother of God. She'll hear you when no one else will."

Thus Alma the long-standing agnostic led herself through this imagined dialogue and then, to kneel on the red-carpeted hotel room floor and pray to the Virgin Mary for comfort, for courage, for strength to see herself through this trying time. As ridiculous as she always thought the teachings of the Church, still, it was comforting sometimes to pray, to pretend that she believed in the Lord Jesus Christ and that his mother, the Blessed Virgin, who truly loved and understood women, would put in a good word for her.

As she prayed her agitation ceased (did the drug the doctor gave her wear off?), and she was flooded with a warm feeling of peace and well-being. Now she knew she would be all right. "Thank you, Blessed Virgin Mary," she whispered, "thank you," and got up off the floor. She'd feared she would flip out, undergo a complete breakdown of some kind, and what do people do when they undergo such a thing? They fling themselves out of windows. Off bridges if they can find one. She was grateful, to whom or to what she wasn't sure, just grateful that she'd somehow moved back away from the edge with her life and sanity intact. But what would she do now? What would she do with the long hours left before the time came to board her plane and go home?

Just minutes ago she'd been on her knees praying to Mary, whom she didn't even believe in, so desperate was she . . . . And now, now that her wish had been granted and the anxiety lifted, she felt she had to set about finding some way to occupy herself. She opened the drapes and looked out the window. Some boys had a bicycle and were taking turns riding it up and down the sidewalk. Did they have just one bike among them? she wondered. It was a beautiful day, if a bit too hot. Her nose suddenly began bleeding as she stood at the window looking down at the street below, at all the cars and people, the boys riding their bike. It was such a glorious day. She soaked a towel in cold water and held it to her nose and lay down until the bleeding stopped, then she changed her clothes (she'd brought enough clothes to last a week—she didn't know why). Alma rode the elevator down and walked out onto the street, intending at first to go for a walk . . . but Mexico City was so big and busy and if she got lost how would she make her way back?

She noticed several taxicabs parked in front. The driver of one asked if she would like a tour of the city. Three hours, just twenty American dollars. She reached in her purse and pulled out a twenty and handed it over to him and he opened the back door for her and she stepped inside. It was an old car, very old, probably as old as herself.

He took her to see mansions belonging to rich Americans and to see hovels on the side of the hill made of scrap wood and tin signs, several painted a pastel blue or green, orange or pink. Some of these, in addition, were marked with five linking circles, the symbol of the Olympic Games that had taken place in Mexico City the year before. "It was a great time," the driver told her. "One American couple commissioned me for the duration and I accompanied them to the games. I was paid well. I got to see the Olympics." Her nose began to bleed. This time she was prepared for it. She'd brought a towel from the hotel to hold to her nose, and it didn't bleed very long or very hard.

"Did you hear about the big plane crash at the Mexico City airport? The day before yesterday. Everyone killed. No survivors. A big commercial jet. What do they call them? 747s?

"A good sign, señorita. It means another will not occur for a long time." She knew it didn't. It didn't mean anything.

He took her to the university to see the mosaic murals. One huge mural showed a man, whose coloring was light tan, reaching down and towards the other side where a woman with brown skin stood reaching up and towards the man. In the center of the mural the man and the woman held, between them, a baby that was

◄○►
Alma

lighter than the mother but darker than the father. The cab driver told Alma that this mural depicted Mexico, the infant (cuter than either of its parents), whose father was Spanish, whose mother was Indian. Finally, just before they had to go back to her room to get her luggage and then to the airport, he took her to see the pyramids.

Before the Spaniards came to Mexico (in search of El Dorado or whatever, in search of eternal youth, maybe they thought the gold could buy them that), a great city, an Indian city stood on the site of modern Mexico City. These pyramids belonged to those long-ago Indians. Alma felt some sort of connection to these Ancient Ones. Right before her eyes was tangible evidence that they lived. The pyramids were built by the ancestors of the modern Indians own hands, structures where they worshipped their God or gods, who were fierce like all ancient gods, so fierce they might require human sacrifices from time to time. What were they, these people? Mayan, Incan, Aztec? Alma knew very little about Mexico and its history. But hadn't Mayans been the people, like the Greeks, whose civilization was so advanced? Poetry and art, medicine, mathematics, architecture. And hadn't the Aztecs been, like the Romans, superior warriors who had defeated every Indian nation, including the Mayan, and appropriated everything? These pyramids were most likely, she thought, built by Aztecs. They built tall structures because they'd wanted to be closer to God, to the sun which they believed was God. What would they think if they could see the Empire State Building? As Alma stood looking up at the stone pyramid, rain began to fall, gentle, warm, tropical rain, and the light all around her turned golden-rose.

She wept a little in the car on the way back to the hotel. Her nose started bleeding again and she had to hold a Kleenex to it and put her head back. She didn't want the driver to see her weep. He might ask her why and she would have to make up something (like, when he asked her what brought her to Mexico City, she'd said she'd come for a very short vacation, a little sight-seeing trip was all). She didn't feel like making up anything or discussing why she wept. Besides, she didn't know why. Were her tears shed for the baby that she left in Mexico? Or, rather, the potential baby, the beginnings of one? Maybe this baby would have been greatly loved and Alma would have thought things like *Thank God I didn't go through with that abortion. She has been such a joy to me!* The struggle would be so hard, though. If she had had another child, would the three of them, her boy and the new one and herself, have had to live on welfare, become trapped the way government reports say people are trapped generation after generation barely subsisting on welfare, not having enough to break out, just enough to keep alive? Who knows what would have happened had she given birth to her second child? She tried to remember the face of the man whose bed she woke up in, who had made her pregnant when she was drunk, "Hey, Seuss." A thin man in his thirties with shaggy hair and beard. What would she have told her child about his/her father? He died in Vietnam? He died in a car wreck? Something. She wished she hadn't married Lennie, that she and James, especially James, who idealized his Daddy, never had to see his damned face. She didn't want another baby. Not now. She was only twenty years old, not many years when compared to the age of the Aztec pyramids. What was even one lifetime compared to them?

A Spanish version of a familiar American song played over the speaker system in the airport. Alma wondered if the Spanish words said the same as the English: *You can dance every dance with the guy who gave you the eye; let him hold you tight . . . but don't forget who's taking you home and in whose arms you're gonna be. So darlin', save the last dance for me.*

From then on, even when she heard it in French as she would on her car radio when she was forty-one and driving through Quebec, she would remember her trip to Mexico City.

Now the song made her think here she was twenty and divorced and she didn't have anyone to take her home, no one in whose arms she was going to be. Would she ever? Would she be alone all her life? *Music's fine like sparklin' wine go and have your fun.*

Flying home to San Francisco, the bright moon didn't seem any closer than from the ground. She saw its reflection in a lake far below. The lake, which she knew was a large one, appeared to be only slightly larger than the moon. And the full, white moon's reflection filled the surface of the dark lake and there fiercely shimmered.

◄○►

Alma

* * *

Coyote loved a beautiful young woman named Frog who loved a poor boy named Badger to whom her father would not give her hand until he had established himself and could support a wife.

Coyote was obsessed with this beautiful maiden. He had to have her for his wife. He went to Frog's father and asked for his daughter's hand, offering twenty horses. Frog's father turned him down. Coyote was not respectable, not a person of good character, known far and wide as a liar, a coward, a thief. Not many would regard him as good son-in-law material. Coyote contemplated this problem and, after awhile, came up with an idea: Frog's father, a prudent and prosperous man, had one terrible weakness: he loved to gamble. Coyote went to Frog's father and said, "My heart is broken that you will not give me your daughter's hand, perhaps you will do me a kindness and play me a few games. It would console me if you would." Nobody could gamble against Coyote and win, everyone knew, but Frog's father accepted the invitation.

They gambled into the night, all through it, into the next day. When Coyote had won all Frog's father's horses and blankets and everything he owned of value, Coyote let him gamble on credit and Frog's father went deeply into debt. Coyote left Frog's father alone for a few hours to let him think of the fix he'd gotten himself into.

When Coyote returned, he made Frog's father an offer: he would not take any of what he had won and would forgive the debt, and would even give the old man six of his finest horses if he could have Frog's hand in marriage. Frog's father, with a heavy heart, agreed.

That very day the old man announced his daughter would wed Coyote on the night of the next full moon.

Frog was broken-hearted. Her father told her there was no getting out of it. He'd given his word and that was that.

Frog went down to the river, to the flat rock that hung over the water where she and Badger secretly met. Badger, having already heard the bad news, was already there waiting in the shadows. When he saw her approach, he called her name, "Frog, oh my dear Frog!" and she ran to his embrace.

The two lovers lay on the rock and pledged their undying love for one another as they often had. "Whatever will we do?" they said and wept in each other's arms. They talked of suicide, they talked of trying to kill Coyote. Finally they came up with a plan: Frog was to pretend to accept her fate. On the night of the wedding, when she would be left alone in the teepee right before the ceremony, she was to go ahead and put on her wedding clothes, then take her knife and cut a tear in the back of her teepee and slip through it to the path that went down the hill to the river. Badger would be waiting for her with two horses packed with all they would need to begin a new life. They knew they would then be alone, no longer a part of any tribe. It was a price they were willing to pay.

Frog kissed her boyfriend one last time, then left him sitting on their rock in the moonlight, and he watched her until she disappeared under the trees. Then he returned to the village.

Under the rock, unknown to the lovers, Water Snake lay the whole time, listening to their plan. Snake slithered off to tell what he'd heard to his friend Coyote.

The night of the wedding arrived and everyone believed Frog's act, or appeared to believe it. When she was left to spend her last hour as a maiden alone, Frog dressed herself in the beautiful white buckskin dress all bedecked with designs of colored porcupine quills. She put on her leggings and moccasins, braided her freshly washed hair. She heard the drum begin, and the voices of the singers rise. When they finished their song she was supposed to emerge from her teepee. She took her knife and slashed a tear in the back of the teepee and stepped through it.

The full moon lit the summer night nearly as bright as day. Frog ran down the path she'd traveled so many times before, knowing this would be *her last time. She ran through the woods and to the rock that was her and Badger's secret place, but when she got there, standing on the rock, a big grin on his face, was Coyote.*

"You look lovely, my dear. What's wrong? Were you expecting someone else? Not that boy Badger, I hope. I had him killed." Frog turned around and began hopping back the way she came, Coyote chasing close behind, calling to her, saying, "Come back, dear Frog. I love you. I'll make you the happiest woman in the world." Then Frog realized she ran in the wrong direction and turned around. Coyote thought she'd changed her mind and was coming back to him. He closed his eyes and opened his arms wide to embrace her, "Oh, my darling," he sighed, but she hopped right over him, landing on the other side.

She ran and hopped as fast and as high as she possibly could away from Coyote while he pursued and begged her to come back. Higher and higher she hopped, more and more out of control, but not caring. Finally, she hopped so high she landed on the moon.

If you look carefully, when the moon is full, you can see Frog. She's still there. And when Coyote howls at the full moon, you know why he howls. He's lovelorn still, after all this time, and pining for his little lost love.